Funky Lily's Shorts

*A delightful collection of short
stories and essays*

Lilian Marton

Note for Librarians: A cataloguing record for this book is available from Library and
Archives Canada at www.collectionscanada.ca/amicus/index-e.html
ISBN 1-4251-0814-8

*Printed in Victoria, BC, Canada. Printed on paper with minimum 30% recycled fibre.
Trafford's print shop runs on "green energy" from solar, wind and other environmentally-
friendly power sources.*

TRAFFORD
PUBLISHING™
Offices in Canada, USA, Ireland and UK

Book sales for North America and international:
Trafford Publishing, 6E–2333 Government St.,
Victoria, BC V8T 4P4 CANADA
phone 250 383 6864 (toll-free 1 888 232 4444)
fax 250 383 6804; email to orders@trafford.com
Book sales in Europe:
Trafford Publishing (UK) Limited, 9 Park End Street, 2nd Floor
Oxford, UK OX1 1HH UNITED KINGDOM
phone +44 (0)1865 722 113 (local rate 0845 230 9601)
facsimile +44 (0)1865 722 868; info.uk@trafford.com
Order online at:
trafford.com/06-2572

10 9 8 7 6 5 4 3

Table of Contents

DEDICATION

First and foremost, I want to dedicate this book to my dear husband and loyal partner of many years for his unconditional support of whatever new project I undertake, no matter how madcap it may seem to others. Thank you, George, for your patience, for never putting any restrictions on me, for giving me honest feedback whenever I ask for it, and for getting me out of some inevitable computer jams while assembling this book.

My gratitude also goes to the ladies of my monthly writing group who have always been supportive and encouraging. If it hadn't been for the 'pressure' of having to produce and read new material at every meeting, my writing might not have been so prolific. Thank you for all your feedback and suggestions over the years.

Last but not least, a heartfelt thanks to a former English professor at my university who had told me in no uncertain terms that I could NEVER be a writer because my mother tongue is not English. His condescending remarks were my greatest motivation.

Thank you all!

Lilian Marton.

INTRODUCTION

Life is short, and at my age it's getting shorter faster than ever.

That's why, after years of writing for newspapers and businesses, I finally decided to get back to my short stories and essays and share them with the world at large.

This book is a personal history sprinkled with fiction, told in short stories or in essays with often independent themes, exposing my inner thoughts, but all reflecting and exploring life experiences, events and feelings—some significant and insightful, others humorous and whimsical—all acutely observed. Some are written using my anagram, Mollina Tarin.

At my first Creative Writing class at university back in the 1970s, the professor told us that we each had to write 18,000 words between September and May. While other students groaned at the prospect, realizing that this was not going to be the easy course they had hoped for, I thought: Yes—I can do that! As soon as I got home after class, I hauled out my small, portable typewriter and started writing. For the next few hours I sat at the kitchen table and typed out the draft of the story that had been weighing heavily on my soul for so many years. Once I started writing, I could not stop. The experience was incredibly cathartic—the words kept tumbling onto the page. It was as if that nightmarish experience of long ago had been waiting to be vomited out, finally, and the relief was instant. That's how *Death of a Dog* came out into the open.

More stories followed. Another professor had started publishing the stories of some students in a bound volume every year, so I approached him to find out if I could submit one of my stories. He listened to my accent and laughed. "You'll never make a writer," he said. "Your mother tongue is not English—so how do you expect to ever know the language well enough to write a story?" Annoyed, I replied, "No, English is actually my fifth language, but it's my working language. Don't you even want to read one of my stories?" He laughed again. "No, I don't—I told you, you'll never make a writer!" And with that, he showed me out of his office.

Well, I just kept on writing, and before even graduating I started working for a newspaper, then for the university, and for the next 25 years I made my living writing. In addition, every life experience became potential grist for my mill of stories and essays. For example:

Have you ever wondered why healthy people die in their sleep? Then consider a startling but plausible reason given in *Dream Yourself to Death*.

Survive a hurricane on a tropical vacation in *Innocence Lost*.

Want to pass time with Walter Matthau and Carol Burnett at their funniest? Check out *LIGHTS! CAMERA! ACTION!*

Have you *Danced With a Clown Today?*

Choose Your Life Philosophy may tempt you to try and influence your life span.

How does it feel to have lived in three different centuries, all in one lifetime? *Millia Vara, Centenarian*, can enlighten you.

Throughout this book I have attempted to sort through the clutter of life by questioning and trying out different perspectives, bearing witness to human foibles and the oddities of life—lives full of compromise and improvisations, searching for the bigger picture. From touching to funny to thoughtful, there is something for everyone.

Welcome to the wonderful world of Funky Lily. Joyful reading!

Lilian Marton
a.k.a. Funky Lily the Clown
a.k.a. Mollina Tarin

Author permission at: funkylily@aol.com
Website: www.funkylily.com

PHILOSOPHICALLY SPEAKING

The mind, once expanded to the dimensions
of larger ideas, never returns to its original size.
(Oliver Wendell Holmes)

Never An Empty Road

Back in my impressionable teenage years growing up in Switzerland, after spending some unfortunate years in a foster home, I had a scary vision after observing some very boring adults: I realized that the worst thing for me would be to look back on my life at any time—and see an empty road!

Right then I decided that I would never get stuck in "neutral" as long as I had a choice.

Well, my life has been anything but an empty road so far. Luckily for me, I learn easily, and I am intellectually curious about almost everything, so I have managed to do most of the things I love ever since I was old enough to make my own decisions.

My mother passed her travel bug and common sense on to me, and my multi-lingual father gifted me with language facilities, and that combination made traveling anywhere so much easier and more enjoyable.

If my family had not been so poor, I would have trained to become a dancer. But there was no money for a music or dancing career, so I decided on the next best thing: I became a ballroom dance teacher because the studios train qualified applicants for free.

For five years I taught hopeless clodhoppers how to look graceful on a dance floor, how to lead almost any partner into any dance step, how to behave like gentlemen no matter what. Yes, it is possible to turn a man with two left feet into a Fred Astaire wannabe: some men simply require a lot more time and patience to get to that point. But such transformations are unbelievably rewarding for a teacher! Although it was a poorly paid, physically and psychologically demanding job, it was easily the work I loved most. And, after a long day of teaching from 1 to 11 PM, we teachers then went dancing: that's how bitten we all were.

In Canada I also discovered University degree night classes that had not been available in Switzerland. Working full-time during the day and studying at night for years, I graduated with a B.A. Cum Laude in Journalism and a minor in Cinematography in 1979, opening more doors for me.

Since my first full-time writing job in 1974, I realized that writing was the ideal profession for an independent and free spirit like me, because a writer never gets bored—no two writing assignments are ever the same. Every job is new and different. Whether I wrote for the government or corporations or a university or a tabloid, or freelanced for magazines and newspapers and charities, or was commissioned to write specific books, or indulged in short stories and essays, it was always a different experience.

In addition, as I had decided to learn or do something new

every year in order not to stagnate, my attention also turned to other things. I dabbled in filmmaking, immersed myself in Yoga, practiced Reflexology, gave workshops to seniors, and I'm still involved with Reiki, an ancient Eastern hands-on healing modality that also helps me to further my spirituality.

Then, a chance meeting with an actress on a cruise got me involved with local talent casting agencies. With so many films being made in Toronto, there is a constant demand for extras or background performers, and I ended up working in many films and TV shows around town, giving me yet another exposure to a different and interesting world.

Later, an article in a local newspaper led me to a clown course being given by a group of professional clowns, and I thought: Now there is another thing I have never done! And thus Funky Lily the Clown was born, along with Funky Santa, providing me with an exhilarating liberation I had never realized was possible. As soon as I get into costume, my whole persona changes. My inner child emerges with such an infectious exuberance that automatically embraces people of all ages. It never ceases to amaze me that my clowning can make so many people happy while I'm having such fun!

One thing is sure: I never want to stop learning, and I will never allow life to be boring. After all, boredom is a choice, and it will never be mine. As Anthony Robbins puts it: "If you do what you've always done, you'll get what you've always gotten."

Looking back on my life I detect a pattern of stepping stones to further my life's purpose: helping enrich people's lives with consumer information writing, workshops, teaching them skills, bringing healing into their lives with Reiki, or creating more joy with my clowning.

My life an empty road? NEVER!

*   *   *

A Clown Is Born

In the middle years of my life, much to everyone's surprise including my own, I suddenly gave birth to a clown.

"Funky Lily" came into the world fully grown, with an unruly mop of long, mauve hair, and an exuberance that was hard to match. I did have advance warning, however. For some time I had heard a muffled inner voice trying to make itself heard, telling me that I was growing much too serious—a result of an often challenging life.

"Don't you realize that you never had a childhood?" the voice reminded me. "Don't you think it's about time to let me out to play and enjoy myself?"

That started me thinking. True enough, when I was little, childhood was a luxury my family couldn't afford to give me. So when the muffled inner voice kept nagging, "Hey! Let me out of here!" I decided that it was never too late to have a happy childhood. But why should I wait until I was senile?

What a liberating experience it was to develop an alter ego that allowed me to let go of my inhibitions—within limits, of course—and let my inner child out to play!

That inner child turned out to be a clown. WOW! I brought up Funky Lily to be a "jollyologist" spreading jollity and carefree cheer and joyful nonsense whenever she gets the chance, be it among the young or the old, in hospitals or nursing homes, at Christmas parties and other charity events. She is an active and interactive walk-about clown, dancing with whomever wants to dance, doing balloons and telling stories with puppets.

Her storytelling also started another inner assault. "You have so many stories inside of you—what are you going to do with them?" Funky Lily kept nagging me. "Are you going to take them to the grave with you?" What an unbearable prospect! You should never die with your music still in you. So she persuaded me to organize my stories and let other people read them.

In the meantime, learning is always a must, and Funky Lily had some learning to do. When you look up "clown" in the dictionary, you may find such explanations as cartoon character, buffoon, performer, fool, or comedian—it can even be an awkward, clumsy, boorish fellow, a bumpkin with coarse manners. However, a good clown is an artist, a performer who can make you laugh, lift your spirits, and always take a positive approach to make you feel better. Funky Lily already had the basic clown prerequisites: a zest for life, a cheerful disposition, a positive attitude, and a natural 'funny bone.'

So I sent Funky Lily to clown school to learn the essentials, like the Clown Code of Ethics—basically a set of rules of common sense and good manners. For example:

Lose your self-consciousness, but never your temper.

Never do or say anything offensive to or about anyone.

Always be friendly and courteous and respectful.

Make fun only of yourself—never embarrass others.

Never smoke, or drink alcohol, while clowning.

Avoid sexual or religious jokes.

Be aware of personal hygiene, especially sweating.

Sense and respect a person's own space.

A clown character must originate and develop from within you—even your puppet comes from within you. Maybe that's the secret of good clowning: you cannot pretend to be what you're not, WITHIN.

That's also where the art comes from: the art is YOUR truth. And your truth can make clowning an art.

As the mother of a clown, I'm happy to say that Funky Lily is an artist.

*   *   *

Choose Your Life Philosophy

Is it possible to change your life philosophy and, in the process, change your life expectancy? Let's explore that idea.

The web site www.deathclock.com may sound morbid, and at first glance it seems to take itself rather seriously, but it's actually fun to play around with it.

The introduction says: "Welcome to the Death Clock, the Internet's friendly reminder that life is slipping away... second by second. Like the hourglass of the Net, the Death Clock will remind you just how short life is."

To view your Death Clock (or anybody else's), you simply complete the fields in the form shown on the screen: your date of birth, sex, smoking status, mode, and BMI. To determine your BMI or Body Mass Index, you enter your height and weight, and your BMI number will appear which you then enter on the form.

Then you click on "Check Your Death Clock" and there is "Your Personal Day of Death" with a clock ticking away and counting down the seconds you have left to live, be they in the trillions or only in the thousands.

Well, to test the system, I entered the information of my 96-year-old mother-in-law who, in 2004, is in good health in a nursing home, but has shrunk away to just a tiny human being. With her current height and weight, she showed a BMI of 17 which is no longer part of the scale, the lowest number being 25.

Anyway, I checked her death clock, and here is what it said:

"Your Personal Day of Death is Friday, September 4, 1987.
0 Seconds Left to Live."

And a separate message drove home the point: "I am sorry, but your time has expired! Have a nice day!"

Hmmm… verrry interesting!

So, of course, I checked my own, which showed my "Personal Day of Death" to be August 21, 2013. On my friend's birthday? In nine years??? Well, if that was the case, I had better start getting all my affairs in order and get a lot more traveling done…

However, I got curious about the "mode" line that is automatically set at "Normal" and checked out the other possibilities listed to see if they made any difference. Well -- again, verrry interesting!

Here are the differences regarding my own 'scientifically calculated' demise when using the four different available modes:

o When set at Normal, I check out on Wednesday, August 21, 2013
o When set at Optimist, it's Wednesday, October 20, 2032
o When set at Pessimist, it's Wednesday, June 22, 1994
o And when set at Sadist, it's Tuesday, August 21, 1973

So, if I consider myself 'Normal,' I only have another nine years to enjoy life. But if I'm an Optimist (which I am to a large extent), I have another 28 years to go—good God, NO! Considering the way the world is developing, I don't really want to stay around that long! So my life expectancy should be somewhere between Normal and Optimist, which is a timeline I'm willing to handle. But, in any case, I'd better be careful with those Wednesdays…

However, as a Pessimist, I would have died 10 years ago (self-fulfilling prophecy in such a case?), and as a Sadist I would have died very young indeed and presumably saved the world a lot of grief.

This raises an interesting possibility: Can we change our life philosophy in order to choose our life expectancy? Can we switch from Normal to Optimist in order to live longer? Can we "commit suicide" by switching to becoming utterly pessimistic? Can a person who is prone to depression try to become more optimistic and thus live longer—maybe a lot longer?

I suspect that this wonderful theory may not be as simple in practice as it appears. Wishful thinking alone will not cause a Pessimist to switch to Optimist; that's where psychologists may help. And Optimists may not want to "commit suicide" even at the worst of times.

But if you want to have some fun with that theory, decide what mode you are—Normal, Optimist, Pessimist, or Sadist—or what mode you would want to be, and then try to adjust your life philosophy accordingly. After that, I suppose it's a matter of 'wait and see' whether this affects the 'scientifically calculated' date of your projected demise.

Good luck!

(2004)

A License To Live

My husband, ever the pragmatic philosopher, asked me the other day: "What do you do on the sixth day of an eight-day vacation?"

Not quite sure what he was getting at, I shrugged my shoulders. "That would depend, I guess," I answered vaguely, waiting for him to enlighten me.

"Well—imagine you're in Acapulco, and you've been relaxing and taking it easy on the beach and by the pool, just enjoying the sunshine," he said. "You've seen the most important things and done some shopping. But now it's the sixth day, and on the eighth day you have to leave. So—what would you do?"

Following his train of thought, I said, "I would draw up a list of things I still wanted to do and see, and schedule to do and see them before departure."

"Exactly," he said, beaming. "You're getting my idea!"

Still not sure where he was heading with all that, I waited for him to continue. After an appropriate pause, he did.

"I've decided that we should treat life the same way," he finally said. "I'm past sixty, which means I've started the sixth day of my eight-day vacation, so to speak. Although I may well live beyond eighty, chances are that I won't be able to enjoy as many things in my eighties and beyond.

"Therefore, my sixties and seventies are the sixth and seventh day of my eight-day vacation, for all practical purposes."

I liked the brilliance of his idea. "You're right!" I said. "After all—in the eighties, with a few exceptions, we may all just sit around in the departure lounge, waiting for the flight home," I added.

He got up to get a notepad and pen. "So let's take stock of the things we still want to do and accomplish and enjoy while we can," he said. "And this list will be our license to live."

*   *   *

Dream Yourself To Death

Every once in a while, I read in the newspaper that someone

"died in his sleep" and I think: that's how I would like to go. Just like that, no illness, no accident, no pain—just go, in my sleep.

But why do people die in their sleep? It's not a heart attack. They are not necessarily old enough to have simply 'worn out' and died. There is no obvious physical reason that caused the death.

Well, here is my own personal theory. No facts, no proof, just a theory that can never be proven, but a theory borne out of some very strange dream experiences of long ago.

Dream #1

It seemed like a regular day in secondary school. Nothing memorable happened; the teacher was droning on about some subject or other. Suddenly there was a strange, uncomfortable breeze in the classroom and a tall, gaunt shadow appeared at the window.

A horrible sense of foreboding gripped the students and they started to scream. The shadow moved into the classroom and we all recognized it: it was the grim reaper, with scythe in hand. Very tall, his skeleton rattling as he moved along, he began to mow down the students, systematically, one by one, and they dropped to the floor, dead, under their desks, one by one. Nobody tried to escape.

"Oh no—I'm not yet ready to die," I decided. "He's not going to get me. I'm going to outsmart him this time." As he was cutting down the students in the row next to me, and getting ahead of me, I quickly moved over into the first row where the students were already lying dead under their desks. I quietly dropped to the floor, assuming a dead posture, blending in with the dead students, trying not to breathe noticeably. With bones rattling eerily, Death kept moving systematically along the remaining rows until all the students were mowed down, dropping dead below their desks.

I did not move; I held my breath.

Finally, Death had finished his task and was looking around the room to see that nobody was left standing. The whole thing had taken only a couple of minutes. He started moving toward the window to leave, but stopped as he reached my body. Had he discovered me? Had he sensed my body heat, or the wild beating of my heart? I lay there motionless, among the dead students, afraid to breathe, afraid to look.

There was dead silence.

Suddenly I heard the swoosh of the scythe. Death had sensed my life, and he was going to terminate it, now. I was, after all, going to die, right now, at this very moment.

Instead, I woke up.

Dream #2

I was walking along the beach somewhere, alone. The ocean was still and gray; there were no swimmers, no people, no ships. I was alone. I was not lonely; there was no sentiment attached to my being alone. I was at peace with myself.

Suddenly I came across a baby carriage in the sand; it was empty. I sat myself into the carriage and started wheeling myself out onto the water, the way one would wheel oneself in a wheelchair, moving the wheels with the hands, except backwards.

Somehow I knew that I would be able to wheel myself across the water right to the middle of the ocean, and I was not afraid. I also knew that, once in the middle of the ocean, the carriage would begin to sink, and still I was not afraid.

Once I arrived at the middle of the ocean, the baby carriage began to sink, very slowly. At this point the ocean was obviously deepest, so it would take a long time for the carriage to reach the ocean floor. Somehow I also knew that, once the carriage and I hit bottom, I would die.

Slowly descending in the water, I tried to remember what I had read about drowning deaths: a certain sweetness, an intoxication. But I felt nothing. No sense of intoxication, no choking, not even fear. If there was water in my lungs, it did not bother me; it was natural. I just sat in my carriage, waiting to hit bottom.

Suddenly, a gentle jolt. We had touched the ocean floor, and I expected to die, right now, at this very moment.

Instead, I woke up.

Dream #3

I found myself in a situation of self-defense. The assailant was facing me, a brutal man with a weapon in his hand. With my back against the wall, I could not run away; I was afraid, because I would not be able to defend myself in any way. The man lunged forward and thrust a large knife into my gut. The pain was almost overwhelming. I tried to stop the bleeding with my hands, but there was too much blood.

Would I die? Maybe not, if the assailant would now leave me alone, and if I could get to a hospital. At that moment the man took out a gun and shot me in the chest. Did he hit the heart? I was not sure, but even if he didn't, I would not be able to survive such pain and such a loss of blood.

I felt myself fainting: too much pain, and all that blood... I knew that I would die, right now, at this very moment.

Instead, I woke up.

Conclusion

The question nobody will ever be able to answer is:

IF I HAD NOT WOKEN UP, WOULD I HAVE DIED?

Would I have been one of the statistics who die in their sleep? "But she was young and healthy—there was no reason for her to die, in her sleep or otherwise," people might have said. And nobody would have known what caused my death. I would have remained one of those mysterious deaths that doctors and family could speculate about for years to come.

After all, people who die in their sleep never came back to tell us what happened. Had they died in their dream and not woken up? If so, why not? Did their dream create such stress on the body that it simply gave out? Did they have a sub-conscious death wish that was being fulfilled in their dream? Or did they, at the crucial moment, realize that existence on the other side was better?

Why did I wake up? Don't misunderstand me—I'm not complaining: I'm definitely not ready to die yet. So, does it mean that my body is strong enough to withstand the stress of a death dream? Or is my desire to live simply so much stronger than such stress?

I'm afraid that once I know the answer, I won't be able to tell you about it, because I will be in the great beyond.

*   *   *

LIGHTS! CAMERA! ACTION!

I always wanted to be somebody, but I should have been more specific.
(Lily Tomlin)

Hollywood North

Toronto has often been called Canada's "Small Apple" because of the vigorous arts and theatre scene. But just as often it is referred to as "Hollywood North" because of its thriving film industry. Countless films are produced here because of our plentiful supply of excellent actors and competent film crews. Torontonians can get confused downtown when street names and business signs are changed to reflect New York or Chicago or whatever foreign locale is needed for a film. There are also numerous talent casting agencies providing an unlimited number of background performers and extras willing to work in films and TV shows being shot around town.

For more than three years I enjoyed doing just that, working with some well-known stars shooting at least part of a film in Toronto. Many of those jobs were 12-hour shoots, sometimes overnight, especially when the filming took place in a location occupied otherwise during the day. The titles were often just working titles that could change once the film was finished. A number of those films were destined for HBO, so I never got to see them. Here are some examples of films, among many others:

The Fixer with Jon Voight had to be shot Sunday and overnight because the Civic Center would see hundreds of civil workers streaming in again Monday morning. The huge hall was needed to accommodate not only the stars but also 108 background performers, all dressed up at their chicest, portraying Chicago's rich crowd at a party celebrating a new airport mega-project.

Heaven Before I Die was a 13-hour overnighter at a famous Inn and Restaurant/Club, with Andy Velasquez playing the Chaplinesque Jacob of the JACOB AND THE PIG story, and with Omar Shariff playing the Lebanese poet Khalil Gibran.

Happy Face Murders was another 14-hour overnighter at a Roadhouse on the outskirts of town, featuring Anne Margret as a frumpy-looking housewife and Nicholas Campbell as the suspected murderer. The pilot for the TV series *Nothing Too Good for a Cowboy* was another overnighter, but outdoors in a country club, as told in the story TRUE HORSE POWER.

The pilot for *West Wing* of DINNER AT THE WHITE HOUSE was a 12-hour all-day Sunday shoot at the University of Toronto Club that was not occupied that day.

Some other memorable stars I worked with were Kim Basinger in *Bless the Child* with Jimmy Smits; Jane Seymor, whose nanny brought her just born twins to lunch at our restaurant while filming *Absolute Truth*, with William Devane; funny man Martin Short in *A Simple Wish* where I played one of about 100 Fairy Godmothers at an international convention of Fairy Godmothers; Kyra Sedgwick in *Critical Care* with James Spader; Ed Harris as a priest in *The Third Miracle*, along with another 9 priests and some Arch Bishops; and, of course, Walter Matthau and Carol Burnett in *Marriage Fool*, as in the story WALTER AND CAROL.

*   *   *

Walter And Carol

"Oh, you look perfect! Don't change a thing!"

Wow! What an uplifting way to start the day, I thought. I looked at the lady approaching me, a lady I didn't know but who turned out to be the wardrobe person in charge.

I had been told to bring a few changes of wardrobe reflecting a Hawaiian theme. I had nothing Hawaiian, so I brought everything I had with flowers in it, which wasn't very much as I prefer solid colors. But it seemed that what I wore was perfect.

Most women had brought appropriate clothing, while some drab-looking men were given colorful shirts to wear. About 40 of us were to attend a Hawaiian theme party as part of the film, "The Marriage Fool."

Finally we assembled in the dance hall, some getting fake drinks at the bar, others inspecting the buffet table with fake fruits and fake sandwiches and cakes, still others sitting at round tables surrounded by fake palm trees lining the dance floor. A fake band was playing on stage to recorded music.

Suddenly a whisper made the rounds like a brush fire. An elbow poked me in the ribs. "There he comes! Look!"

All eyes turned toward a slightly stooped older man who was being guided into the hall. Walter Matthau! At age 78, he looked not a day younger. His distinctive facial features were more pronounced than ever.

But wait! There was another, younger version of Walter. About 40 years younger, the same body type and characteristic facial features. It was Carl Luff, his double and stand-in, who had been told to dye his hair black and shave off his mustache for the duration of the film. His duty was to take Walter's place while the space with the lighting and everything was being set up, with Walter getting into the scene only for the actual shot.

But, wait again! There was yet another Matthau look-alike, very young-looking and slim. It was Walter's son Charles, the director of the film. From the back and side he looked like a young Anthony Perkins, but his face was unmistakable Matthau.

It was fascinating to watch Walter Matthau, the great old pro, at work. Everything seemed to come naturally: every movement, every facial expression was funny. He joked with us background performers and was friendly with everybody. The crew always guided him lovingly back to his seat and made sure he was comfortable while touching up his make-up and fixing his hair.

Another whisper made the rounds as his leading lady arrived in the hall. Carol Burnett, at age 64, looked smashing! Very slim and sexy, dressed in flashy orange from head to toe, she was to pick up Walter at the dance. In the story, this is Walter's first outing after his wife died, and he is reluctant and nervous. Carol takes charge and they start dating, and end up getting married despite the family's objections. This is their first encounter.

"Hey," Carol calls to him from the other end of the bar. "What's your sign?"

Walter looks confused. "I don't have a sign—what do you mean, a sign?" he finally asks her. "I used to be an accountant, but I didn't have a sign."

"I mean—Leo, or Aquarius," Carol explains.

"Oh, you mean astronomy," Walter picks up.

"No—that's astrology," Carol corrects him.

They break out laughing. The scene needs to be redone.

"Hey," Carol calls to him. "What's your sign?"

"I was a lawyer in Saudi Arabia, but my sign fell down."

"No—I mean—Sagittarius, or Leo."

"Oh, you mean astronomy!"

"Astrology," Carol says.

"I'm a Libra," he finally says. "What are you?"

"I'm a hooker."

We all burst out laughing, and the scene had to be re-shot.

"Hey—what's your sign?"

"Size 42, I think."

More laughter, more re-shoots. And so it went all day. The dialogue was different every time, always funny, undoubtedly to amuse the crew and the background performers. After all, would the great Walter forget his lines? Finally, after about seven retakes, they decided to play it straight, and the scene was done.

Between the various scenes at the bar and later on the dance floor, it was an absolute delight to watch the interaction between these two naturally funny people. There seemed to be real chemistry.

Whenever Walter's son Charles, the director, wanted him to change something, he put his arm around his father and gently directed him to the correct move. It was very touching to see the genuine affection between father and son, very personal yet staying professional.

After one of the funniest and most pleasurable 12-hour days I had spent in a long time, we all collected our money and left. When the film appeared on television just 11 weeks later, in September of 1998, I was disappointed that I could not relive the many laughs of the filming, because it was not a comedy but a romantic drama.

*   *   *

Walter Matthau died of a heart attack less than two years
later, at age 80, in July 2000. I will always be grateful to have had
to privilege to work with him.

(1998)

Dinner At The White House

There was a congenial atmosphere at our round table, a fairly
even mix of handsome men in tuxedos and perfectly coiffed and
elegantly gowned ladies. Looking around the crowded room, I
noticed that even ugly men looked handsome in their tuxes.

The State Dinner at the White House appeared to be a
success, with the U.S. President and the First Lady, as well as
the Japanese Emperor with his Lady in a kimono, and many
diplomats in attendance.

Dessert was almost finished now, and guests were beginning to
move around, greeting people at other tables. The U.S. President
sat down at our table for a chat, and I looked at him admiringly.
With his lean face, a strong chin line and graying temples he was
very attractive, possibly a ladies' man.

"What's your name?" he asked me across the table.

"Monica," was my impulsive reply. "Have you forgotten
already?"

He looked at me blankly, and caught my meaning only after
other people at the table started laughing.

"QUIET! No talking, PLEASE!" the assistant director
shouted. "I don't even want to hear a WHISPER!"

Chastised, we smiled obligingly and continued mouthing

imaginary conversation until that scene was finished and we were sent back to our holding area.

We were on the set of the 1998 pilot for "West Wing," a new TV series taking place in the White House, the West Wing being the political section as opposed to the Residence. The plot centered around political and other intrigue involving two attractive young women, one wanting to expose the President and the other protecting him.

The filming of this formal State Dinner took place at the University of Toronto Club on University Avenue, an elegant house built in 1929 and lovingly maintained. The holding area for the 120 actors and background performers was unusually comfortable: a lounge with leather chairs and sofas and small signed sketches and watercolors on the walls, and a larger room with fireplace and sofas and round tables, and a collection of large, valuable Group of Seven paintings. Quite a change from the more usual church basements or school cafeterias!

A winding staircase led to a series of more formal, even higher-ceilinged rooms upstairs, with heavy drapes and fancy walls and ceilings with gilded cornices and friezes. In our designated state dinner room hung a huge oil painting of a surprisingly young Abraham Lincoln.

It was a 12-hour Sunday for us, starting with a 7:30 a.m. call time. The wardrobe department had provided me with a long, slim, sleeveless, shrimp-colored evening gown with a lovely multi-hued sheer shawl because my own dress didn't quite reach the floor, and they didn't like my elegant black tuxedo pants. So, all day I was struggling to keep myself from tripping over my 12-foot long shawl because it was too slippery to stay in place for very long.

How much easier it was for the men! They didn't have to carry

a choice of wardrobe with matching shoes; they simply brought—
or wore—their tuxedo. However, a youngish man at my table, a
'48 tall' size, split his pants as he was untying his shoes; he had
to wear his overcoat until he found a kind soul in the wardrobe
department who was willing and able to fix his problem.

Much of the day was spent sitting around and waiting. I was
happy to catch up on a lot of reading, while many others played
cards, or dominos. My '48 tall' table mate was working through
his "Windows '95 for Dummies" book, while another man was
sprawled across a sofa, snoring contentedly.

"The President and the Emperor: UPSTAIRS!" commanded
the assistant director. "I also need the security men, with your ear
pieces, and all the floaters—upstairs, right now!"

"The floaters?" I asked my table mates. "What does that make
the rest of us—sinkers?"

As the entire building was a smoke-free area, the hard-core
smokers had to borrow umbrellas to satisfy their cravings outside
in the continuing heavy rain.

At one point, the relative silence was interrupted by insistent
chanting outside. As it turned out, about 300 placard-carrying
Serbs were demonstrating next door in front of the U. S. Embassy,
and the lone policeman guarding the Embassy had to call for
reinforcement. Within minutes, about 20 police were dispersing
the rain-drenched demonstrators, and the usual Sunday silence
fell upon University Avenue again.

"I need the dancers and all background performers upstairs—
now!" We wound our way down the hall and up the stairs, carefully
stepping over the heavy cables and past the camera and lighting
equipment, and sat down at our designated tables.

A few select, elegant couples were now dancing to softly
swinging music. The camera concentrated on one attractive,

young couple that seemed surprised at meeting each other at this State Dinner.

"I didn't expect to see you here," she murmured sweetly. He just held her tightly and they continued swaying.

But after a short while she stopped. "Tell me—does your job require you to carry a gun in your pocket?" she asked him. "Or are you just happy to see me?"

We groaned. "What a tired old line!" my handsome escort muttered under his breath. "And we'll probably have to listen to it another ten times, what with all the retakes!"

Indeed, we sat through several more repetitions before that scene was a "print" and we were sent back to our holding area.

"That's a wrap!" it was announced. "Make sure you return everything to wardrobe before you get paid!" It took me a while to remove the special transparent double-sided tape that had kept my bra straps from showing, but finally—finally!—I was on my way home, a little bit richer.

(1999)

Jacob And The Pig

There was an almost reverential hush in the elegant room as the fifty or so high society guests waited for the last note of the short but exquisite Flamenco concert to waft away before breaking into appreciative applause. The handsome, young guitarist on the small stage bowed modestly, but couldn't hide his proud smile. It was such an honor for him to perform for this elite group.

The guests were mingling again while sipping their after-dinner coffees and brandies. It was an older crowd, distinguished men in tuxedos and black ties, and elegant ladies in evening gowns exhibiting their best jewelry. There were well-known bankers and politicians and business tycoons. My escort pointed to a tall, slim, white-haired gentleman: a judge, he whispered.

At this point, our gracious hostess came back into the salon, shaking a few hands, stopping to say a few words here and there. Then she walked up to the small stage and announced:

"Dear friends—I have another surprise for you!

Ladies and gentlemen, please welcome

JACOB AND THE PIG!"

All eyes were fixed on the door next to the stage where a tall, skinny, Chaplinesque young man was trying to make his entrance. His oversized black pants were tied securely at the waist with string, his back jacket was too tight, his black mustache twitching just the right way. A black hat and cane completed the vision. On the way up the steps to the stage Jacob tripped over his giant shoes but caught himself with his cane.

But that's where the Chaplin resemblance ended. With his free hand he was pulling a reluctant pig on a leash—very reluctant because the poor pig's hoofs kept slipping on the steps. But finally it was standing next to Jacob on the stage, large and very pink, looking freshly scrubbed, snorting happily with a great sense of accomplishment.

But—oops—what was that smell? A few brown heaps made their appearance on the stage. Some of the guests close-by turned away in disgust, others held their noses. How piggish!

"CUT!" yelled the director. A slight, wiry man named Isidor rushed up to the stage. "Somebody clean that up! Where's the trainer?"

A woman appeared with a pail and a roll of paper towels. She stooped and scooped and erased all evidence, then gave the pig a couple of handfuls of lettuce and disappeared again.

"OK—let's take that again—everybody back to their places," Isidor said, and the film cameras got into position again.

But there was that smell again! Another few brown heaps appeared on the stage. "Trainer!" yelled Isidor, still patient at this point. The woman with the bucket went through her routine of stooping and scooping again, removing all traces off the stage, feeding the pig a handful of licorice. This trainer obviously believed in the reward system.

"Do any of you ladies have any Chanel 5?" asked Isidor. "We have to do something about that smell!" Nobody volunteered. "OK—somebody get some Lysol spray!" A gofer rushed out to find some Lysol and sprayed the stage area with it.

"OK—let's try that again," Isidor sighed, and people went back to their positions.

The pig, however, wasn't ready to relinquish his role as star of this production. But this time the brown heaps were accompanied by a steady stream of urine.

"TRAINER!" yelled Isidor, exasperated now. The woman went through her familiar routine, but as she was ready to reward the pig with more licorice and lettuce, Isidor commanded, "No more feeding! This is costing me too much time and money!"

Finally the stage was cleaned up once again, Lysol spray wafted through the salon, and cameras and the background people were back in their places.

"This performance should be called 'Jacob and the Pooping Pig,'" whispered a lady next to me, and we were trying hard to stifle a laugh. "SILENCE!" shouted the assistant director. "No talking—only mouthing, PLEASE!"

Jacob went through a short clownish routine, while his pink pig behaved remarkably well, doing nothing. As the mismatched pair got off the stage, with tripping feet and slipping hoofs, the guests crowded forward, clapping enthusiastically. The hostess got on stage to thank the performers, while we kept clapping.

"Cut! That's a print!" yelled Isidor, relieved.

We sat down in our easy chairs in the holding area and discussed the time lost with the pooping pig. It was three in the morning, and we had more scenes to shoot. These scenes were to be part of a film called "Heaven Before I Die" with Giancarlo Giannini and Omar Shariff, released in 1997.

Finally, by six a.m., the salon scenes were finished. All the background performers headed back to the small ballroom where we had left our bags and wardrobes. We all lined up to get paid for the 13 hours we had put in. Then some people changed back into their jeans, while others headed for their cars in their evening clothes, trying to beat the morning rush hour traffic.

(1996)

True Horse Power

It was a cold, clear night, with a brilliant three-quarter moon moving slowly across an indigo sky. Although it was the third week in April, the temperature was still well below freezing, causing all the high-class party guests in the garden to shiver, even in their coats.

"De-coating!" came the command, and we reluctantly shed our coats and handed them to the gofers that quickly hid them away from camera vision. We tried not to rub our hands or shiver too much and pretended to enjoy ourselves at the elegant garden party in a country club setting in a make-believe Vancouver summer.

All the ladies were wearing old-fashioned hairdos and

make-up, and summer evening gowns provided by the wardrobe department, as this was a 1939 setting. We were freezing! At least the men were able to wear long underwear under their tuxedos, but the gentler sex just had to suffer the sub-zero temperatures, some in off-the-shoulder dresses and fancy sandals.

"There is too much breath! Can we get some ice?" the director yelled. Ice? I didn't know about the others, but no way was I going to chew on ice to eliminate my steamy breath! I would rather stop breathing, I thought. It already took all my concentration and willpower to keep from shivering too visibly… But, mercifully, no ice could be found at this time of night.

"Cut!" The gofers came running with our coats which we hastily put on, and we all started stamping our feet in a futile effort to warm them up a bit.

Whenever a particular scene was finished, after whatever necessary number of retakes, we were allowed to go indoors again to thaw out.

On a 12-hour all-night shoot, such as this one, one tends to sit at the same table with the same people during breaks, for long stretches at a time. Some are reading, some playing cards, others writing essays for an upcoming exam, still others napping. Invariably there are 'wise guys' trying to show off their experience and imagined knowledge, ending up sounding like silly jerks. "If he had kept quiet, he might have retained his 'nice guy' front," the lady next to me whispered knowingly, pointing to a loudmouth.

This production, called "Nothing Too Good For A Cowboy," was to be a pilot for a planned TV series, and showed a young high-society woman falling for a handsome cowboy at a ranch next door. At some point, a run-away horse crashes the party at the country club, scattering the guests. The handsome young cowboy rides through the garden club, trying to reign in the panicky horse, and with the help of the young lady manages to open a closed gate to let the horse out, much to the relief of the guests.

Now the next scene had been set up, and we had to get back outside to our outdoor places again. On the covered patio, four musicians and a singer were entertaining the guests with danceable old tunes from the '30s. Tables were set up on a large terrace in front of the patio and along a walkway lined with a cedar hedge, leading to the closed gate.

The musicians, of course, were only pretending to play and the singer was mouthing the words to recorded music. The cedar hedge consisted of potted cedars, the pots being hidden. The walkway was narrowing as it got closer to the gate, and my table was the last one before the gate.

"Rolling!" The runaway horse charged through the dancers and down the walkway, with the cowboy riding close behind in pursuit. The guests were scattering between and behind the tables without much prodding.

As the runaway horse reached the closed gate just past the last table, it panicked and started circling right in front of my table, looking for an escape. His giant rear end was only about three feet from my face as it swung around with unexpected speed, close enough for me to feel its body heat, its huge eyes glaring at me accusingly as it swung back. Genuinely scared, I backed into the cedar hedge, almost falling over the pots. A wrangler materialized out of nowhere and calmed the horse down to lead it back to the beginning of the scene.

"Cut!" This scene was repeated several times, and I decided to remain standing behind the table, close to the hedge, just in case. One gentleman in tuxedo at my table advised me to dive between two pots, if I felt in real danger, as there was enough room behind the hedge to accommodate my escape. He turned out to be one of several stuntmen, experienced with horses, located strategically along the horse's path.

As we were all freezing again, we were allowed to spend some time indoors to warm up before going back to more of the same. The bass player was moving his beautifully polished instrument back inside, complaining bitterly.

"If I had known that we don't have to play, I would have just rented a cheap bass, instead of bringing my own valuable one," he grumbled. "This temperature fluctuation from freezing to warm is really damaging!"

The other musicians didn't have that problem. The pianist was pretend-playing an old upright piano that hadn't been tuned in years and, with some keys missing, was totally unplayable anyway. The silent drummer and saxophonist only had cold fingers.

Now it was time to continue filming the same scene again, but this time with the young lady running alongside the cowboy and calming down the runaway horse, then opening the gate to let it out. She sure knew a few things about handling horses! Some of her young well-heeled friends were following behind on foot, commenting on this unexpected distraction.

"Rolling!" But at that moment, the runaway horse stopped, lifted its tail and produced a neat heap of beautifully braided manure. "Shovel! Shovel!" a few people shouted, but the director was more to the point. "Get the steamers out of here!" she yelled. "Yes—can you bring them to my rose garden?" somebody joked.

Finally, the steamers were removed and shooting resumed, but we had lost valuable body heat time with our coats off.

Several times the tuxedoed stuntmen among the guests along the pathway had to handle the runaway horse whenever it got too close to the tables or too threatening to any guests. Even so, one table got knocked over, sending the plastic glasses flying. And the scene had to be retaken.

Every time the horse was charging past my table and I was faced with the giant rear end again, I pressed hard against the hedge behind my table, trying not to fall backwards into the hedge, hoping to remain safe. This spectacular demonstration of true horsepower impressed me every time, despite my equally true moments of fear. But I decided that I much preferred such horsepower under the hood of my car.

Finally, all the scenes were shot to apparent satisfaction, and we sat around indoors, getting warmed up and drinking coffee or hot chocolate, and devouring more cookies and chips. We ladies still needed to drink through straws so that we wouldn't wear off the special dark lipstick that was apparently worn in 1939, just in case we were called out again for a re-shoot.

All night we had needed to be careful with food and drinks, because the make-up people didn't have time to redo all of us after every bite. So we kept drinking through straws and breaking up our food into small bites, unable to eat the beautiful apples that are always provided in large quantities. After our main meal, which we were able to eat normally, we all had to go through make-up again for touch-ups and that special lipstick.

"That's a wrap!" This was our release call, and we all changed back to our 1997 clothes and tried to take all the hairpins out of our elaborate old-fashioned hairstyles. The excessive hair spray could be washed out at home only. The female stars peeled off their false eyelashes to give them back to the make-up people. All the old-style dresses and shoes were returned to the wardrobe department.

Then we lined up to get paid and headed home as dawn was breaking, beating the morning rush-hour traffic.

(1997)

A Real Hobo

Who would have thought that spending time with a hobo on a movie set could teach us a valuable lesson about discrimination?

No, I'm not talking racial discrimination; much has been said about that already. But how about social discrimination? How often do we judge others by how they dress, or behave? And every time we judge, we discriminate.

Just recently I caught myself judging and discriminating again. When I was working in a film called Flesh and Blood, I spent a long day in a run-down area of the city, and part of the film involved hobos and prostitutes.

When I arrived on location early that morning, the small park around the church where the action was taking place was still full of homeless people. Some were huddled in their sleeping bags on top of picnic tables and benches, others on the ground, leaning against the walls of the church or nestled in corners. I had never realized that so many homeless people were spending their nights in even such small church parks.

As the film crews were setting up their equipment, I asked one of the assistant directors whether they would use those hobos in the film.

"Some of them, yes," he said. "The others are extras."

In the holding area where all background performers have to pass through the wardrobe and make-up departments and spend their time waiting, and where refreshments and meals are served, some down-and-out street people were sitting around, waiting. They were delighted to spend some time indoors, to belong to a group if ever so temporarily, and to fill up on coffee and snacks and later on a full meal.

Without being too obvious, I scrutinized them, trying to discover whether they were real or made-up. Their clothes were torn and stained, their faces and arms dirty, and even the skin showing through the holes in their dirty T-shirts was dirty. I did not go close enough to any of them to find out if they smelled or not. Some had obviously been in fights, with scratch marks on their arms and evidence of fistfights on their faces. Since nobody could tell the difference, the tendency was to stay away from any hobos.

Were they all real? Or were they fakes? I had no way of telling, short of asking them. But, how would you ask? "Excuse me, Sir, are you a hobo, or an extra?" Obviously, I could and would NOT do that!

Then I asked myself: WHY was it so important for me to know? Would I treat them differently, if I knew? Would I consider the real hobos less valuable as human beings? And if so, was that not gross discrimination?

Back out in the park, I spent more than an hour talking with a hobo on a bench as part of a background scene. Fred was a scruffy-looking man with a slight build and wispy hair. I was really intrigued with his thinking, although I could not figure out whether he had recently escaped from an institution, or whether he was just quirky. Very earnestly, he was informing me of the second coming of Christ in 2010, and how we must do everything to be prepared for that eagerly anticipated event. Wondering where he got such information and to keep the discussion going, I challenged him on the date, suggesting it might be 2012 as some people believe, because the Mayan calendar ends at 2012. He looked at me wide-eyed, impressed that I seemed to take him seriously.

It was during that conversation that I realized that Fred was a

REAL hobo: he had teeth missing. The extras made up as hobos simply had some teeth blacked out, something you could see only in a close-up. But my bench friend clearly had teeth missing, and that was his give-away.

When that scene was finished and we were asked to return to the holding area, I was genuinely glad to have spent time with Fred the hobo, and I suspected that a conversation with a 'regular' extra might not have been as stimulating.

Any reluctance on my part to interact with him would have deprived me of such an unexpected experience.

(1998)

A WONDROUS WORLD

*The world is a book, and those who do not travel, read only one page.
(St. Augustine)*

Windjammer Ahoy!

Sailing to exotic islands on the Polynesia, a genuine old four-mast schooner, has an irresistible appeal to the adventurous side of my Gemini nature. But my more rational side reminds me that I can get seasick watching home movies.

"Seasickness—a rarity aboard large sailing schooners, since the wind on the sails prevents a rolling motion," assures the Windjammer Barefoot Cruises brochure. But I buy a large supply of Gravol, just in case, and proceed (via New York and Puerto Rico) to St. Maarten in the West Indies from where the Polynesia sails every Tuesday.

One may become an official "stowaway" on the windjammer the night before sailing. A modest supplement buys a Welcome Aboard Party with rum swizzles and snacks to get to know the barefoot crowd, a dinner, barefoot dancing under the stars to a local steel band, the first queasy night in the small cabin, and the Tuesday breakfast.

A motley crew will share the ship's fairly restricted space for the next six days, for better or for worse. By the Tuesday noon sailing, I count about 90 heads ranging from teenagers to sexagenarians, from families with their youngsters to sophisticated singles.

There are two decks for frolicking. The upper deck is devoted to sunbathing during the day and sleeping under the stars at night—and, incidentally, for hoisting and lowering the miles of sails.

The main deck houses the vast dining hall that can usually serve the meals in one sitting, and the ship's well-attended watering hole. The bowels of the ship can sleep up to 126 people in cabins that accommodate from two to six people each.

After lunch we all gather on the upper deck to witness or participate in the first hoisting of the huge sails. Many of us are photographing the event while the more physically inclined get behind the ropes, about 20 deep, to pull in unison. The Polynesia has four masts, each almost 200 feet high, and the rigging is appropriately complex.

Suddenly we hear the roar of the wind in the full sails and the ship, now listing a permanent 15 degrees, is urged forward.

Hair aflutter in the breeze, I adjust to a leaning-tower-of-Pisa body position and savor the unbelievably exhilarating feeling of having suddenly merged with nature, of being one with the sea and the breeze and the sun. With this natural high, who needs rum swizzles?

We're on our way to Nevis, a tiny, unspoiled jewel of an island in the Caribbean. The Polynesia—affectionately called the Poly—is scheduled to visit Anguilla, Saba, St. Bart's, St. Kitts and Statia the first and third week of each month, and Antigua, Guadeloupe, Iles des Saintes, Montserrat and Nevis the second and fourth week. But these islands become quite interchangeable, depending on wind conditions.

In practical terms, the windjammer is a floating no-frills hotel since the one- or two-week cruises are really island-hopping excursions. Most of the sailing is done overnight to allow for more time on the different islands.

Passengers are invited—but not necessarily encouraged—to lend a helping hand with deck chores, learn about rigging, and stand wheel watch. Of course, we all have our picture taken at the giant wheel!

Captain John Green briefs us on the hazards of sailing and gives us the dos and don'ts of windjamming. First Mate Vyvyan Jones offers informal lectures in celestial navigation and seamanship twice a week.

Mealtimes become a social experience with 10 people seated around each table in the dining hall. There are free Bloody Mary's and hot rolls for the early risers at 6 AM; a more copious breakfast for the late sleepers is served until 8:30 only. Lunch is shortly after noon.

Free rum swizzles and snacks at 5 PM will hold us over until dinner at 7:30 when free wine is served. A 'midnight' snack appears around 10:30 PM because, by midnight, most passengers have hit their bunks, tired from a busy day of dolce vita. Free hot coffee and tea are available 24 hours a day, but libations from the bar require cash.

It's 'story time' each day after breakfast on the upper deck. The captain's daily briefing informs us about the day's island, what to see and what to avoid, where to shop and when to be back on the Poly for sailing.

After Nevis and Montserrat we sail to Antigua, a trip that takes 16 hours because unfavorable wind conditions force the Poly to tack (zigzag) all the way. My Gravol pills forsake me, but swimming at Antigua's glorious beaches helps me, and others, forget the uncomfortable night.

After the entire day at Antigua we dance to a local steel band on board the ship until we hoist the sails for our last stretch to St. Bart's.

Tonight many of us stay on deck to watch a fantastic performance of meteor showers. With this heavenly display, together with the breathtaking sunsets and the delicately iridescent sunrises we've witnessed every day, we windjamming city folks will just never be the same.

After St. Bart's, the last night aboard we enjoy a farewell gourmet dinner with French onion soup, lobster, Caesar salad, cheesecake, champagne and liquors. This is followed by a joke-swapping session on top deck where Captain Green, all spruced up in his naval whites and fluffed muttonchops, shows his skill as social director.

Slowly we realize that we have fallen under the spell of this romantic, beautiful ship. We have become attached to the friendly crew, to the jolly yet aloof captain, to the Poly's informal barefoot atmosphere.

And as we drag our luggage off the ship back on the island of St. Maarten Sunday noon, we forget about the floating stomach and the sand fleas on deserted beaches.

We are sure of one thing: we will be back on a windjammer—except that next time we will have to pay. This trip I won free in a contest!

(1978)

Innocence Lost

Acapulco, one of Mexico's most beautiful and popular tourist destinations on the Pacific coast, lost its innocence when

Hurricane Pauline devastated the port city in October 1997, claiming well over 100 lives, leaving tens of thousands homeless, many missing, and probably thousands more deprived of their livelihood.

For most locals, this was their first hurricane ever, and it traumatized them beyond belief. "So far, the storms always stayed off-shore, and we always just got wind and rain," explained Miguel, whose small boat lay broken in a newly created gully on the beach, among broken trees and beach umbrellas and piles of garbage. "This is the first time it hit the city—the first time we have dead people and such damage."

A gray-haired man in his seventies sat in a damaged boat trying to empty the water out of it, cup by small cup. He looked sad and hopeless, and shook his head. "What will I do now? I guess I'll have to start all over again," he said, with tears in his eyes.

"No, we have no insurance—none of us can afford insurance," he added. "Besides, this is an Act of God. They wouldn't pay."

In a designated area for vendors, some shacks had collapsed onto the beach as powerful waves had undermined the retaining wall. The owners were sifting through the rubble that used to be their business, trying to find anything salvageable among the broken furniture and twisted cables and grotesquely muddied Styrofoam dummies clad in shredded bathing suits.

Some vendors were luckier. Merchandise stored off the floor and well covered with plastic and tied to pillars survived intact, and they only needed to shovel the foot-deep mud. Within hours they were open for business again. But many vendors found much of their merchandise damaged.

Nearby, some concrete steps leading to the beach lay collapsed and broken, perhaps hiding yet another body.

The miles of famous beaches were littered with mounds of all manner of garbage washed in from the ocean, including thousands of plastic bottles of all sizes and colors. It looked as if Mother Nature had finally gotten sick of the thoughtless pollution and had decided to vomit it all back.

Entire sections of beach were washed away, leaving large craters filled with broken boats and beach paraphernalia and uprooted trees, with an occasional dead dog. A blackbird was hobbling on one leg, the other leg twisted and broken.

As far as the eye could see, the water of the bay was brown and muddied, unfit for swimming for days to come, although on the second day the pleasure boats were driving by empty to show that they were ready for business, even in pouring rain.

The cruise ship that had arrived in the harbor the day before was now securely anchored in the middle of the huge bay, waiting out the storm. Had it remained in its usual place in the harbor, the storm would have tossed the ship against the pier and damaged or destroyed both.

The usually crowded Costera Miguel Aleman, the wide boulevard lined with shops and hotels and restaurants, had become a river of mud and could be crossed only barefoot, preferably with a long stick to probe the depth of the water and mud. On the second day some buses ventured out, having to make unexpected detours as major intersections were still not navigable. The roads leading down from the surrounding hills had become raging rivers of water and mud, dragging along trees and boulders and houses and sometimes children and dogs, flooding the lower sections of the city with mud and debris and blocking the intersections.

The underground tunnel leading from the hotel zone to downtown Acapulco was filled with mud and rocks and garbage, trapping some cars with their occupants that were later found dead. Underground garages were equally impenetrable, with cars completely buried. Vehicles parked on streets or sidewalks were smashed against walls or pillars, or ended up on top of each other.

The unprecedented disaster brought out the best and the worst in people. Spontaneous and impressive solidarity could be seen everywhere. Some skinny young boys were trying to dig a stuck Jeep out of the foot-deep mud with bare hands, while the well-fed tourist driver stood by smoking his cigar, not wanting to get his hands dirty.

With many roads and the airport closed, the shortage of food and drinking water and gasoline and medicines soon became evident. Certain merchants began doubling or tripling the price of basic necessities, and photos of arrested looters appeared in local newspapers.

"My daughter is getting married Saturday," said Javier, a taxi driver who had escaped the worst. "I hope the people can get to the church—an empty church would be a bad omen!" He discreetly wiped his eyes and walked away.

Tourists experienced minor inconveniences. Most hotels generated their own electricity, although not enough for air conditioning, and the food and water supply was interrupted. Some insensitive tourists complained about having to eat pasta again, or not being able to use the beach that was full of craters and garbage, or the swimming pool that was now full of sand, or about the beauty salon being closed. All the while locals were still digging for bodies, trying to find missing family members, or waiting for basic necessities in the many shelters being set up for the now homeless, or trying to identify bodies in the temporary morgues set up across the city.

After two days the airport opened again, during daylight hours only, and tourists had their return flights delayed accordingly.

Telephone service was practically non-existent for two days, and worried families back home waited anxiously for a sign of life. Tourists on longer package tours were given the option to be bused to Puerto Vallarta via Mexico City, or fly home early.

The beaches came alive with scavengers young and old—locals digging through the almost unbroken line of garbage, looking for something useful. One of the beach's regular stray dogs was searching in vain for her recent litter. Hotel staff started cleaning up the tons of debris on the beach. Life resumed in a paradise lost.

Roberto, an unemployed musician, was staring at an Acapulco he had never seen in his 56 years in this city. "It is so terrible—so terrible," he sighed. "I have not worked all summer, and I was hoping to play again in the high season, this winter. I have a family. But now, maybe we will not have a high season…"

In the meantime, my friend and I, both of us now hurricane survivors, had experienced six days of the best and two days of the worst the paradise of Acapulco had to offer.

(1997)

A Broad Mind

They say that travel broadens the mind. But understanding and speaking the local language can turn a simple, 'mindless pleasure' vacation into a fascinating, compassionate and eye-opening experience.

My mind really got stretched beyond expectations when I, a confirmed Mexican enthusiast, decided to take advantage of an incredibly cheap one-week, all-inclusive package tour to Cuba.

Not only did it include three meals a day and all local alcoholic beverages, but also (for those interested) a crash course in devastating poverty, hunger, political propaganda, intimidation, fear of police and imprisonment, lack of freedom under a totalitarian regime, general hopelessness, and total deprivation of off-shore news.

Intimidation

After having undergone the usual sufficient luggage inspection upon departure in Toronto, it was an unwelcome demand from Cuban officials to open and totally unpack my suitcase upon arrival.

In front of the whole tour group, I had to justify every item in my carefully and methodically packed luggage, from underwear to books to toilet articles. "A book?" the officer asked, glaring at me. "Yes, I like to read." When a few minutes later he found another book, he demanded, "Why another book?" "Because I like to read, and I'll have time to read," I replied patiently, trying not to sound exasperated—I didn't want to start my vacation in prison. At least he didn't confiscate my books.

This crude invasion of my privacy left me struggling for polite cooperation with my uniformed Peeping Tom who, in the end, could find nothing objectionable. To my question (in Spanish) what he was looking for, he just shrugged his shoulders. "Nothing specific. Just looking." Seeing that I was upset about the whole thing, he looked at me apologetically when his supervisor wasn't watching and dared to whisper to me, "I'm sorry, but I have to do this."

It is also possible, of course, that these men were simply curious to find out what seemingly affluent foreign females own and use. But it left me with the impression that I was entering a police state—an impression that was later reinforced when we had our passports confiscated for a day and were issued a hotel guest ID card.

Fear of Police

Although it is natural for tourists to tip in American dollars when warranted (the use of U.S. dollars is strongly encouraged), locals are forbidden to own foreign currency. In fact, anyone caught with U.S. dollars risks going to jail. Under the same law, locals with U.S. dollars (from tips) are not allowed to set foot inside a hotel store—which would be the only place for them to spend that currency—or again risk jail.

Where does that leave your friendly Cuban workers who are trying so hard to give you good service? Those desperately poor Cubans who are counting on tips for some extra income and hoping that tourism will be their economic salvation?

As I soon found out, they have to rely on cooperative tourists who will buy the necessary items for them in the hotel store.

As word got around that I was a trustworthy specimen who also spoke Spanish, I was approached by various hotel employees who entrusted me with their 'illegal' tip money, along with specific sizes and colors for their needed shirts, jeans, sneakers or anything else they couldn't buy on their own. Of course, every exchange of money or merchandise had to be done very discreetly: none of us wanted to get caught.

"We know that there are employees who were hired to keep an eye on others and report such activities," one musician told me. "But we don't know who these government spies are. So we have to be very careful—we can't trust anybody!" Then he whispered, resignedly, "Son las leyes de nuestro país!" (These are the laws of our country!)

Temporary workers who don't have access to tourists or who don't speak English need contacts with 'runners' who do.

Walking along a fairly deserted beach one day, my friend and I were suddenly approached by three young people. "Please, please, can you help us?" The young woman looked around furtively, while her two male companions stayed half-hidden under the trees, anxious not to be seen by the regularly patrolling, uniformed, armed police.

Expecting some con game, we guardedly asked for more details. In fairly good English, she explained that the two men had some U.S. dollars that they needed to spend but were not allowed to. Continuing to look out for police, she reached into a surprising hiding place on her body and extracted 14 cleverly hidden, folded dollar bills.

"Please, can you buy two shirts in the store? They cost $7 each. Please?" Entrusting me with the money, she then gave us the sizes and preferred colors. All three of them stayed hidden on the beach while we bought these items in the hotel store. When we later handed her the shirts, she again made sure nobody saw her take them before disappearing back into the trees.

Peso at Par

Cuban pesos can only be bought at official exchanges (banks or hotels) at official rates: one peso for one U.S. dollar. "The Cuban peso is at par with the U.S. dollar," officials will tell you proudly. But in reality, the peso is not worth very much. On the street, one could buy between 20 and 40 pesos for one U.S. dollar, but that also carried a jail term for anybody caught in such a transaction.

Musicians working for hotels are among the best-paid employees. They earn about 200 pesos per month, working 12-16 hour days, playing in the dining room for all meals, starting at breakfast, and ending after 11 PM when the nightly stage entertainment ends.

"I make seven pesos a day," one musician told me, "but a package of cigarettes will cost me eight pesos!" He should not complain: his wife, a secretary in a government ministry, gets a whopping 60 pesos a month.

What News?

During my entire stay there, I tried to find a newspaper to keep up with happenings in the world. Every day the hotel clerk would tell me, "We didn't get any today—but tomorrow for sure!"

On an excursion into town in a minibus—a rarity as there is a constant fuel shortage—I searched in vain for any newspaper. Did any exist? "Oh yes—of course we have newspapers," they would answer my query. "But not today." When I did find a bookstore, it contained nothing but political books and propaganda material. No other books or newspapers.

Finally, one of the hotel staff trusted me enough to tell me, "We have such a shortage of newsprint that most of the time there are no newspapers. When there is paper, we get a government propaganda newspaper. No—there is no freedom of the press here!"

Hidden Poverty

Although officially there was no unemployment or poverty in Cuba, we encountered a number of homeless people who, being unemployed, had no place to call their own. They slept along the deserted stretches of beach hidden under big, leafy trees bearing lots of small, green grapes they called 'sea grapes' but that were not edible.

As our hotel dining room served three buffet 'meals' a day,

some of us ended up taking food supplies in our pockets down to the beach daily to the hungry, homeless people who really appreciated our small tokens. Because breakfasts always consisted of the same kind of bread and sliced, yellow cheese and not much else, there was not much variety for them either. Other meals were cooked and not practical for transporting, but we managed to take some baked goods and an occasional fruit whenever we could. They appreciated every bite.

Then one day I saw the young woman 'runner' in the dining room who had asked me for help at the beach. She was with Ted, a man who had always taken pockets full of food down to the homeless on the beach. As it was forbidden for any local to be in the hotel, Ted had officially paid for her to stay in his room for three days, giving her a rare chance to take baths and get hot meals and some new dresses. He didn't mind the disapproving glances of other guests who regarded her as an opportunist, but for him she was charity, and both were happy and satisfied.

*   *   *

Coming from a truly free country such as Canada, my mind was really broadened on this trip, resulting in heightened compassion for a people trying to make the best of living in the iron grip of a seemingly never-ending dictatorship.

Since then, Cuba's President Fidel Castro has eased up on the foreign currency restrictions, making it easier for locals to spend their well-earned tips legally.

(1992)

A Lesson In Bargaining

After countless trips to various parts of Mexico to practice my Spanish, I thought I had more or less mastered the art of bargaining, and I had developed my own philosophy about it.

For example: I don't believe in getting the lowest price necessarily. I love the Mexican people, and I know that an extra dollar saved is worth much more to that Mexican vendor than it is to me because, to him, it may mean being able to feed that extra mouth at home or buy some other necessity.

Even today, the average regularly employed Mexican only earns the minimum wage that is much lower than in our country. A self-employed vendor, on the other hand, has to rely entirely on what he can sell, and therefore he will try to get the best price for any of his wares.

Either way, our affluent North American lives always appear obscene to me in comparison with their daily struggle. That's why I simply decide what an item is worth to me, and that's what I'll pay, unless the vendor offers it to me for less.

But now I have discovered a new twist in the bargaining process.

We had just finished a three-hour guided tour around the famed Mayan pyramids at Chichén Itzá on the Yucatan peninsula, and we had about 15 minutes for shopping before heading back to the tour bus.

The souvenir stalls are conveniently located between the site and the parking lot, of course. I didn't have much money with me, probably less than 50 new pesos. What I really wanted was a T-shirt that, back at our hotel, cost an outrageous 45 pesos.

Suddenly a tiny, middle-aged Mayan vendor held up a wooden statue he was working on and asked me, "Wouldn't you like this one?" I stopped because I'm a sucker for wooden carvings. I picked up the pale, unfinished work and was surprised at how light it was, barely a few ounces.

"Acacia wood," he answered my question in Spanish. He showed me the finished statues painted a wonderful dark chocolate brown with gold and color trim. They were exquisite! Most of them represented the Maya Corn God, a very important God, because corn was so basic to the Maya for both food and trade.

We chatted for a while in Spanish, then he said, "They cost 40 new pesos—but I'll give it to you for 30, OK?" I was mentally calculating how many pesos I had left. If I bought my beautiful Corn God, I would not have enough left over to buy a T-shirt…

The vendor mistook my silence for bargaining, and said, "OK—I'll give it to you for 25!" Wow! Even with this year's newly issued devalued pesos, 25 pesos were less than 12 Canadian dollars at the current 1993 exchange.

Yes, of course, that graceful, elegant, featherweight, foot-high, divine creation would indeed join my collection of wooden carvings from around the world on our mantelpiece at home. The T-shirt would have to wait for another time.

As I was counting out my pesos, I overheard the bargaining going on next to me. "Only 40 American dollars," another vendor said in English to an English-speaking couple admiring the twin brother of my Corn God. "But I'll give it to you for 30."

I quickly calculated that, with three new pesos to the US dollar, that statue had just tripled in price. Phew!

"How much is that in Canadian dollars?" the wife asked her husband. "About 40," he said, rummaging through his wallet. "Yeah—we still have 30 American—do you want it?"

I didn't stay around to find out if they bought their Corn

God. But I had just learned that, at least sometimes or in some places, it pays to bargain in the local language. The price is the same—only the currency changes.

(1993)

Murphy's Law:
Alive And Well In Mexico

Many first-time visitors to Mexico are frustrated at all the things that can, and will, go wrong. However, if you love Mexico as I do, you not only develop a tolerance but actually find these frustrations amusing, a vital part of any Mexican vacation.

On one trip, why did we not get suspicious when our plane stopped on the runway before even leaving Toronto? It seemed that some luggage had found its way onto the plane without an accompanying passenger. And since bags are loaded into the hold in no order whatsoever, it took at least 20 minutes to locate the stray bag in the cavernous bowels of the plane. But finally we were off to the wondrous, fascinating world of Mexico City.

Sitting on a former lake from which the city draws its water, and slowly but dangerously and visibly sinking as the lakebed is drying out, Mexico City has to be seen to be believed. Of course, there are days when it cannot be seen, thanks to a solid blanket of smog that hovers over the city at certain times, the result of thermal inversion due to the high mountains that encircle the city—days when schools are closed in the morning until the sun breaks through to keep the children safe indoors. But the truth be told: during my various visits to Mexico City at different times of the year, I have never suffered from the smog more than I do in Toronto. Of course, I always stay in the city center where there is no industry to worsen the situation. Or is it luck?

Mexico City is a city of contrasts, of beauty and kitsch, of genuine joie-de-vivre and despair, of riches and unimaginable poverty, of modern architecture and archeological treasures, teeming with an estimated 24 million people. It is impossible to take an accurate census because thousands of desperate country people arrive weekly on the outskirts of the city, settling into ever expanding shanty towns up the mountainside, drawn to the unspoken promise of a better life like metal shavings to a magnet.

Taxi, Por Favor!

Taxis are an integral part of a stay in Mexico City. They are affordable, although prices have risen sharply since meters have become a standard fixture in almost all cabs. Before meters, you could bargain and determine a price before getting into the cab; now the price is fixed.

As Volkswagen Bugs were still manufactured in Mexico until very recently, about half of all taxis are Bugs. They are cheaper to buy and run than larger taxis; the front passenger seat is usually removed to give people easier access to the back seat, but they can take only two people. Although the ride is bumpy, you get to your destination quickly and safely. If your money is in short supply, it pays to flag down only Bugs.

Taxi drivers may seem crazy to North Americans, but they are actually very safe drivers, and accidents are extremely few—repair costs are unaffordable for them! Gasoline theft is common, so many taxis will have locks on their gas tanks to discourage gas thieves.

Don't be alarmed if your taxi suddenly mounts the sidewalk. The driver is simply trying to get around an accident site blocking the street, or gridlock—I had never seen real gridlock before! Yes—time is money.

It is quite possible that your taxi driver doesn't know how to get to your destination. This is a very large city, he may point out to you. On one trip, the driver was not familiar with our hotel, so he took us to another hotel in the same area where we could then show him how to get to ours.

On another occasion the driver was cruising around for nearly an hour trying to find the address I had given him. When he finally found it, he was furious when I refused to pay him double the amount we had agreed on beforehand; I had to argue (that's when your Spanish comes in handy) that I was the tourist and he was the driver paid to know the city, and besides, that I was now one hour late for my appointment.

We wondered why our taxi driver ran out of gas during the rush hour on our way to the airport. Simple: his car no longer had a gas gauge. So he just pulled over, filled up his tank from a full gas canister he was carrying in the trunk (another reason they cannot afford accidents—POOF!), locked his gas tank again, and managed to get us to the airport on time.

And what do you do when the door handle comes off in your hand while getting out of the taxi? There again it helps if you speak Spanish: at least you can argue your way out of having to pay for the handle. After all, he may have collected for that handle a few times already.

Let's Try Public Transport

Out of necessity, Mexico City has an excellent public transport system, costing mere pennies to use.

The modern subway, called Metro, carries close to five million passengers a day. During rush hours, certain platform waiting areas are cordoned off for women who prefer the few Metro cars that are reserved for women only, to spare them the experience of getting fondled in the crush of people. However, it seems that not all women want to miss out on that opportunity…

The large, old buses used to be among the major polluters of the city, but they are getting replaced by smaller, cleaner and more efficient buses, some no larger than vans. With a map you can get around quickly and cheaply, and observe daily life in the world's biggest city.

Long-distance buses are equally cheap. For example, to get from Mexico City to Cuernavaca, a charming city in the mountains just 1 ½ hours to the south by modern highway, buses leave about every five minutes from the south-end bus terminal and cost just a few dollars each way.

The mountain scenery along the way is breathtaking, while the warning signs for the benefit of drivers can play tricks with your mind. " Cañón de lobos" warns one. Wolf Canyon? You secretly hope that the wolves are sensible enough to stay off the highway.

"Zona de derrumbes" signals potential rock or landslides, and you hope that the driver will slow down getting into the "curva peligrosa" or dangerous curve ahead.

But the sign that imparts the most colorful impression of Mexican road reality reads: "vehículos sin frenos sigan la raya roja" instructing vehicles without brakes to follow the red line which is painted between the white lines and which slowly runs off the highway into a gravel pit, shortly before the next "curva peligrosa."

While in Cuernavaca, we plan on taking a bus to Taxco, the world-famous silver town further south, clinging precariously to the side of a high mountain. We rush into a nearby restaurant for a quick breakfast, ordering only toast and coffee in order not to miss the bus. While other patrons are served elaborate cooked breakfasts, we finally enquire about our toast. With deep concern they check the toaster, only to find it empty; hurriedly they put in the bread. After another 15 minutes we enquire again. With even deeper concern they check the toaster again, only to find it out of order. At that point we cancel the toast and rush across the street to the bus station.

Wanting to buy tickets, we are informed that the bus has not yet arrived, and that we cannot buy the tickets in advance. While waiting patiently, we try to find out the rationale behind this policy. "Sometimes the bus doesn't come," we are told, "and we cannot give refunds." That explains the confusing bus schedule that lists only the estimated arrival time, but never the departure time.

It seems there are two different bus lines servicing the Mexico City—Cuernavaca sector. On the way back, we want to try the other line. But after waiting an hour for the bus to show up, the station manager finally advises us to go to the other station and take the competitor's buses that leave every few minutes.

Back in Mexico City we are checking in at the airport. The agent at the ticket counter forwards the tickets to the boarding pass counter further down. As we go to collect the boarding passes, my ticket is nowhere to be found. In its place, there is a boarding pass waiting for Mitsuko Yashimoro who had earlier been given mine. With genuine consternation, an agent rushes off into the line-up crowd to find the Japanese man holding the boarding pass of a white woman; luckily they find him before we miss our plane.

The flight back to Toronto is boringly uneventful. After battling Mr. Murphy and his famous law for ten days, life threatens to return to its predictable normalcy once again.

For those of you lucky enough to be not yet familiar with Mr. Murphy's irrefutable law, he said: "Whatever can go wrong, will" or something to that effect.

*   *   *

The Last Meal

We had been trekking through the dirty, dilapidated city of Havana, capital of Cuba, mustering all of our imagination to see the old glory and opulence of what used to be the playground of America's rich.

Decades of communism had taken their toll with a vengeance. The beautiful architecture was now hidden behind crumbling facades and thick layers of pollution. The very visible poverty of the people was depressing because of its utter hopelessness.

Whenever our tour bus stopped to let off our small group of tourists to visit a church or a market, hordes of desperate Cubans crushed against us, pleading, "Jabón! Jabón!"

My Goodness! We were not at all prepared for this. They wanted soap! If we had known, we could have brought our collection of small hotel soaps to distribute. We had been advised to bring extra toothpaste and razors and deodorant, or clothing we no longer needed, to give away as tips, but not soap. The people seemed less happy with just money, because they would not be able to BUY soap with it, anyway.

After a mediocre lunch at what was considered one of the city's best restaurants, we drove across the canal to a lookout point from which we could see Havana spread out below us. A huge cross dominated the square, and armed soldiers congregated in and around a small guard station in the center. An incredibly emaciated small dog was dragging himself around the square.

"Look at that starving dog!" I exclaimed in shock. "He has probably not eaten anything in weeks! How can he still move?"

We checked our bag for some leftover cheese sandwich we had packed at breakfast for our bus trip. Most of the large roll was still intact. We broke it into small pieces and approached the dog. Painfully, he dragged himself closer, and the suffering in his eyes broke my heart. I was close to tears.

We gave him a small piece of bread and cheese to see if he would eat it. He gulped it down quickly, as if afraid that it would be taken away from him. He looked up, and we continued feeding him small morsels that he kept gulping down voraciously. He tried to wag his little tail, but he was too weak. As there was no water around, I squirted some from my bottle onto his nose.

Finally, we ran out of sandwich and started walking away. The soldiers around the guard station had been watching our actions curiously but carefully, but at least not intervening. 'Crazy tourists,' they must have thought, 'feeding a dying mongrel.'

The dog was lying down now, panting, trying to digest his unexpected meal.

"He ate too much, and too quickly," I said to my husband. "Poor thing—he may even die from the overload and the exertion."

"That's possible, of course," he answered. "But at least he would die happy."

*   *   *

Jeeves In Charge—again

Jeeves, the perfect valet of the Honorable Bertie Wooster of

British writer P.G. Wodehouse fame, is alive and well and vacationing in Acapulco, Mexico—or at least he was when I was there recently.

Probably 30 years older than when I last read about him, he is still tall and thin; his face perhaps pinker than I remember, possibly a result of his beloved daily gin and tonic. It also seems to me that his sense of humor is sharper and a bit more wicked, but that could just be a faulty memory or changed perception on my part.

We met one evening before the nightly stage performance in the hotel theatre. "I'm Sheila, and that's my husband Morris," his wife introduced herself with a pronounced British accent.

I stared at Morris. "JEEVES!" I exclaimed with delight. "How wonderful to finally meet you!" And from that moment on, Morris was Jeeves to me, and he played his role to the hilt. "Would My Lady care for a drink before the show?" he asked me with a dignified, slight bow, and with an even stronger British accent. At that moment the lights went out and the show started.

Next day by the pool, Sheila complained to me that she couldn't get a second key to their room, no matter how she pleaded with the front desk people. Her fading charm no longer seemed to work. She realized that 'one key per room' was strict hotel policy, and no clerk was willing to bend the rules.

"Jeeves, why don't you wait until there are only young ladies at the desk," I suggested. "Maybe they are more susceptible to your unique charm and give you a spare key—just tell them that you don't want to be joined at the hip with your wife! That's how my husband always manages to get a second key."

At an appropriate moment later that day, Jeeves came back with a second room key. "It worked!" he announced triumphantly. "They were not going to bend, and I was ready to let it go, when I decided to pout and say, 'but it's my birthday today—so why don't you give it to me as a birthday gift!' So they smiled and gave me the second key!" He hopped around on one foot, swirling the key playfully, then fell happily onto his lounging chair and handed his wife the valuable key.

Sheila immediately decided to take advantage of her new freedom and walked away with a brisk gait that belied her age. "Is it really your birthday today, Jeeves?" I asked him.

"No—not until May," Jeeves admitted. "I'll be 82 in May."

"Wow! You don't look 82," I marveled. "How do you feel?"

"I feel great," he said, looking around to make sure that his wife was not within earshot. Then, with a conspiratorial wink, he added, "Actually, when I'm in the company of a younger woman like yourself, I feel much younger—more like 50. But when I'm with my wife- well, I do feel like 82!"

Our hotel provided a different show in a theatre on the Mezzanine every night. The costumes were spectacular: sometimes glitzy, with lots of sequins and feathers; sometimes skin-tight acrobatic outfits; sometimes elaborate and seemingly authentic folkloric costumes, all depending on the type of show presented.

The performers and the choreography were equally spectacular, totally professional. It was quite a revelation to find out that all performers were employees of the hotel, some hidden away in offices, but most of them working at the pool or on the beach as part of the Activities Department, in Spanish called "Animación." To see these young people so glamorous at night, and then during the day without makeup, in hotel uniforms or in bathing suits, added an entirely different dimension to an already wonderful vacation.

As every night, we had rushed up to the theatre after dinner in order to get good front row seats; it was first come, first served.

Whoever got there first—Jeeves with his wife Sheila, or my husband and I—reserved seats for the others.

As we were anticipating tonight's show, we noticed a small, furry creature, about four inches long, undulating slowly across the carpet between the front row and the stage. When it wasn't moving, it remained in place with just its long, black hair wafting gently in the light breeze of the air conditioning.

All of us in the front row watched it, mesmerized. WHAT WAS IT? How did it get up to the Mezzanine and into the theatre? DANGEROUS? Finally, a child took some timid steps towards it, but within a couple of feet of it ran back to the seat, shrieking. Amid nervous laughter, another curious child moved gingerly forward, only to run back to the seat, screeching.

The creature barely moved, but just kept undulating its lovely black hair. Everybody was waiting for something to happen. Then, a woman tiptoed forward and cautiously bent down without getting too close, then rushed back to her seat stifling a tiny sound of fear. We all giggled nervously and held our collective breath.

Finally, Jeeves rose majestically and approached the creature with the resolution of a man who is used to take charge. Tall, and with great dignity, he stomped his foot down hard and twisted it a few times to make sure that it, whatever IT was, was dead. While everyone applauded, he carefully lifted the thing by the hair and held it up for all to see.

It was a piece of black feather from the costume of a showgirl.

*   *   *

SLICES OF LIFE

The mystery of life is not a problem to be solved,
but a reality to be experienced.
(Aart Van Der Leeuw)

Death Of A Dog

Molly rushed across the village square toward the church, her thick golden-red braids swinging from side to side and her heavy, old-fashioned skirt getting caught between her knees. She saw Alex waiting for her at the church door. He had probably been there for a few minutes already because she was late; it was almost seven-thirty. He pretended to be looking for something in his school bag; he always wanted to make it look as if he got there at the same time accidentally.

"Oh—good morning, Molly," said Alex, feigning surprise. He held the heavy oak door open for her as usual.

"Good morning, Alex," said Molly, completely out of breath.

They entered the dim old church. The faint light coming through the tall gothic windows barely outlined the few people attending Mass during the week; there were mainly school children. As the church was only a stone's throw away from the school, many families obliged their children to attend the short silent morning Mass at seven-thirty before classes started at eight.

Molly was kneeling at the back on the women's side. She felt really grown up because she no longer had to sit at the front of the church with the smaller children since she started secondary school.

Alex was kneeling on the men's side, and Molly felt him staring at her. 'If only he was a little cuter,' Molly thought. Freckles all over his face. Those funny ears—wasn't there something his parents could have done about his ears?

She found this daily Mass terribly boring. She didn't even feel guilty anymore when her mind wandered; she wondered just how many children were actually praying. Sunday Mass was much more interesting because there was music and singing, and the church was always full to bursting. You could watch interesting fashion shows; women seemed to come to church only to show off their new hats and clothes. No self-respecting villager would dare be absent on a Sunday. One had to be seen.

Finally the old priest had finished his mumbling and the church emptied. Alex walked up to the school with Molly; she didn't mind, really. He was a nice boy. After all, there weren't any really cute boys in her class. Thirteen must be an awkward age, she figured. Besides, Hemloch was just a small village.

"Did you have to clean the halls and stairs again before church today?" Alex asked.

"I told you—I have to do that every morning."

"That's silly."

"I know, especially when I have to clean it all again at lunch time."

"They're taking advantage of you, I think," Alex said after a pause. "You shouldn't have to work so hard."

Molly didn't answer. What could she do, even if they were taking advantage of her? She had to stay in that foster home until she finished school. Since her father died several years ago, her mother had to work almost day and night to pay off the massive medical bills he had left behind. That left her no time to look after a school-aged girl. So Molly was sent to stay with this rich family somewhere in the hinterlands and had to endure their quirks. Sometimes it was hard being the only outsider in the small community. Everyone else was born here.

"You know, Stubby snapped at me yesterday," Molly said as they entered the red brick school building.

"Why on earth? Did he hurt you?"

"No, no harm done. We figure it's just jealousy. He's getting old and jealous. They may have to put him down soon."

Molly had mixed emotions about Stubby. When she first came to live with the Hunter family, Stubby was still in fairly good shape for a ten-year-old dachshund. But he was getting fat and had a hard time running. He had now reached the point where his round sausage body was dragging on the ground because his legs were so short.

"I can't use him for hunting any more," old Mr. Hunter had said and had started to look around for a replacement, perhaps a more appropriate dog than a dachshund. He liked to go hunting for rabbits whenever he got a chance. Then, one day, there was a replacement in the kitchen. A fox terrier, very young, very lively, long legs, short wiry hair, black and brown patches all over his white skinny body, a long white tail with a tiny black tip that never stopped wagging. Molly immediately fell in love with him.

The family decided to call him Ringo. He became everybody's favorite; even grim old Mother Hunter stooped to stroke him. Stubby lay curled up in a corner, watching all the fuss about his young rival with a hurt and sadly drooping face, resentful of this new unwelcome presence. Once in a while he growled to make his own forgotten presence known.

How unfair, Molly thought. For so many years he had faithfully served the Hunter family and had gladly been everybody's pet. Countless times he had accompanied Mr. Hunter into the fields and helped him bring home some rabbits. Now that he was old and needed compassion, nobody was willing to give him any. Ringo got all the attention. But when Ringo tried to play with Stubby, all he got was an angry growl, and Ringo had managed to escape an attempted snap more than once. But even with all that, one couldn't just desert old used dogs like that.

Molly crouched down in front of the old fat dachshund. Stubby slowly raised a pair of accusing eyes, then lowered them again. His tail never moved. His attitude made her feel guilty; she was close to tears.

"Stubby, poor dear, we still love you," she tried, but she was aware of the contradiction in her voice.

Stubby growled. She advanced a cautious hand. She wanted to show him some tenderness, let him know that someone still cared. But did she really? Or did she just try to appease that uneasy feeling in her conscience? Stubby had become very unfriendly as of late, sensing the hypocrisy.

As her hand touched the furry rolls of fat around his neck, Stubby's head jerked around in a surprisingly quick movement and his teeth snapped at her. That was the second time now! Shocked, Molly withdrew her hand. There was a spot of blood on it. She didn't know how to react. She was furious that her tentative affection was rewarded with a bite.

Molly stood there, stunned and confused, when Mother Hunter entered the room. There was something impressive and yet intimidating about that erect, matronly figure, about that frizzy gray hair pulled back tight into a severe-looking bun. Although the woman was in her sixties, there was not a wrinkle on her forehead. Molly always had the impression that her skin had grown onto her bones so tightly that it couldn't possibly wrinkle.

"What's the matter?" the old woman asked sternly, her steel-blue eyes flashing.

"Nothing."

"What do you mean, nothing? Then why don't you do some work? We don't keep you here to stand around, you know. What's that on your hand?"

"Nothing." How she loathed and feared that woman. Those yellow spots in the cold blue eyes. The authoritarian voice, always nagging, always criticizing, always complaining. Nothing was ever right, nothing was ever good enough for her.

"Let me see your hand."

Molly instinctively hid her hand behind her back. She didn't want Stubby to be punished.

Mother Hunter reached out and slapped Molly's face. Then she grabbed and inspected the hidden hand.

"Get the iodine," she ordered.

As she disinfected the small wound, she asked, "Did Stubby bite you?" When Molly refused to answer, she muttered to herself, "We'll have to do something about that dog."

A couple of days later, Molly was returning from the fields where she had brought the heavy luncheon basket to some farm hands. That's when she saw old Mr. Hunter tramping through the field, the rifle slung over his shoulder. The grass stood high and Ringo was somewhere in it. As the still handsome man rested his tall, slightly stooping frame against a fence post waiting for the dog, he suddenly saw a few inches of white tail with a black tip moving about in the distance, and his weather-beaten face folded into a smile. Then he saw Molly and waved her over.

"Ringo is doing alright as a hunting dog," he said to her. "Not much discipline yet, but he has a good nose and loves to chase rabbits. Do you like him?"

Molly was very surprised that he talked to her. He and Mrs. Hunter had an agreement that he would be responsible for the menfolk and the farm, and she would take care of the house with the womenfolk and the bakery. Neither would interfere with the other's domain, an arrangement that suited him just fine as he would avoid arguments this way. Everybody knew that his wife was a mean one, and it was safer not to cross her. Now that their five children were grown, he just came home after work to eat and sleep, and spent any other free time hunting or playing cards with his old friends at the only pub in the village.

"Oh, I love Ringo!" Molly enthused. " But—what will happen to Stubby? I mean… "

"I know what you mean… I hear that he's been snapping and even biting, and we can't have that," he said, looking very serious. "But that old dog has been my friend and companion for eleven years, and it will be very hard… " His voice trailed off. "But I must take care of it soon… " And with that, he turned and walked away, with Ringo following him.

Molly wondered if Mr. Hunter would 'take care' of the dog himself, or have someone else do it. And maybe the whole situation reminded the old man of his own mortality, now that he was getting closer to the end... It seemed to her that everything was so temporary, and in a way that was good because she couldn't wait to finish school and get away from this place, this family. Her young mind philosophized that some people, like Mr. Hunter, probably found no justice in mortality, while others, like Mrs. Hunter, would find no justice in eternity, especially if you had lived a mean life.

It was Saturday, the day Molly hated the most. Although she had a lot of work to do every day, weekdays weren't so bad because she was in school most of the time, and she loved school. The teacher liked her because she was bright and learned fast, and her classmates had finally given up staring at her. She had been such a novelty when she first came to Hemloch! A girl from the city—better watch out. City girls are bad, it was said. They talk a lot in school, corrupt the others in class, give them crazy ideas. So for the first six months Molly had to sit in the front row where she could be observed. Not only that, but the girl next to her was quite deaf, and one had to shout to make her hear anything. The teacher didn't want to take any chances with Molly.

Thank God that probation period was over. She had established herself as being quite normal. Some children still called her "carrot head" because of her thick, curly, blonde-red hair that she found difficult to discipline into braids every morning. Sometimes her clothes were laughed at because she wore mostly old dresses belonging to Hunters' grown daughters, and they were too big and too heavy for her just developing figure. But most of the villagers referred to her as 'the girl at Hunters.' She had met many of them on her bread delivery route. Whenever the baker didn't feel like delivering breads with his horse and buggy, it was always Molly who had to go on foot. Or whenever the baker decided it would be too strenuous for his horse to deliver breads to some people up on the hill, Molly was sent to carry the heavy baskets on foot, and if she got back late because she needed to stop for breath on the way up, she would be punished.

Saturday was the day to clean the bakery store. This was such a tedious chore, and Molly hated to be surrounded by all sorts of sweet things that she was never allowed to taste. All the shelves had to be dusted and the parquet floor had to be steel-woolled and waxed. One had to be so careful with the steel wool to stay within the herringbone pattern, not to cross over into the next row, or it would scratch in the wrong direction. When the store was done, the adjoining storeroom as well as the stairs and the two living rooms upstairs had to get the same treatment. Steel wool and wax. Every Saturday, steel wool and wax.

Hunter's oldest daughter, Florence, usually helped Molly in the store because customers had to be served in between. Florence, in her early thirties and still living at home, was tall and angular and ugly and unmarried. She had her mother's cold blue eyes with the same yellow flecks in them. She had also inherited her mother's greed and meanness, and nature had added a goodly dose of cruelty to her already grating disposition.

"She has a long face like a horse," Alex had once said to Molly when they discussed the heartless Hunters, and they had both laughed, although the Hunters were never a laughing matter to Molly. Now that Florence was over thirty, she had the unmistakable look of a spinster about her. With a sour disposition, frustrated and bitter because no man ever made eyes at her, flat-chested and forever nagging, she had less chances than ever to find a husband.

"Why are you staring at me?" Florence asked with a mouthful of pastry.

Molly lowered her eyes and continued to move the steel wool under her feet back and forth. It was so boring and tiring. Florence now stuffed a chocolate bar into her mouth. Molly stared again. How she would love to have some pastry or a chocolate bar or a candy! The store was full of it, but none of it was ever for Molly. Every Saturday when both worked in the store, Florence continuously stuffed sweets into her mouth without ever offering Molly any, and every Saturday Molly resented that greed.

When the job was finally done, Molly got out a large broom and started her other weekly job: sweeping the street in front of the house and the back yard. All residents of the village kept their own stretch of road clean because there were no public maintenance workers. The village was too small.

Curled up in a corner of the back yard lay Stubby. Molly again felt that terrible mixture of guilt and fear and just plain uncertainty. She leaned her broom against a wall to watch him; she didn't dare approach him any more. He didn't seem to tolerate anybody these days.

Florence came through the back door on her way to the barn. She saw Stubby and stopped in front of him.

"You stupid, useless old dog!" she snapped. Stubby growled. For a while, the two faced each other, waiting for things to come. When the dog growled again, Florence kicked him in the gut and started laughing. Stubby winced and trotted away heavily; he was just too tired and disillusioned. Shrieking with laughter, Florence followed him for a few feet, then she turned away to the barn.

All along Molly had not moved, trying to fade into the wall. If Florence knew that she had watched the ugly scene, she would only be punished. Florence was a genius at devising cruel and humiliating punishments, as Molly had experienced herself on various occasions.

'Oh God,' thought Molly, fighting against a sick feeling in her stomach. 'Oh God—I wish they'd let the poor dog die in dignity.'

"You were late today," said Alex as he joined Molly after Mass to walk up to the school. His brown eyes searched her face; he was concerned about her. He wondered what went on at Hunters that perhaps nobody knew about.

Although the Hunters were well respected in the community and attended church regularly where they were known for their generous offerings, Molly seemed to have changed since she lived with that family. A happy girl by nature, she was now often sad and afraid to talk about her foster family, and often he saw bruises on her arms. Sometimes she was even hungry—why would she be hungry when the Hunters were so rich? They owned a big farm and the only bakery in the village. Something was wrong.

"I got behind in my work. Stubby messed up the staircase after I cleaned it and so I had to start all over again," Molly said, then suddenly broke into tears. "They're so cruel with him—I can't stand it!"

Alex was shocked; he had never seen her cry before. "Clean up your face or they'll laugh at you in class," he said roughly, avoiding her eyes.

"What—oh Alex, what do you think they'll do with him?" Molly asked between sobs. "I wish they'd do something... He's getting so -- so mean, doing all sorts of things on purpose. But they really push him to it... they make him do it... they tease him so. And Florence -- I know she enjoys seeing him suffer... Oh, Alex!" The words just came tumbling out of her. "Mean people and a mean dog... Oh, you just don't know how mean they are! What will they do with Stubby?"

"There's not much they can do," Alex tried to console her. He seemed rather at a loss for words. Molly had never really talked about the Hunters, mainly because she felt that nobody would believe her, she had told him, that her status as a foster child had little credibility against such a well-known family. So things had to be really bad for her to break down, he thought. "Mr. Hunter will put him down, or have someone do it for him. That's what will happen."

Wednesday! Molly hummed a happy tune as she skipped home. She always felt hopeful and elated after geography class. All those far-away places—how exotic the whole world sounded to her! Once she finished school, she wanted to be independent, travel and put her feet on all those green and blue and yellow spots on the geography map to find out what people were like elsewhere.

Surely not everybody was like the Hunters. What a frightening thought! Mother Hunter, so cold and stern, always punishing her for something or other: either Molly was too slow in delivering bread, or a tiny speck of dust was found in the corner of a window, or she had soiled her apron a day before the laundry, or she had left her school bag standing in the hall without putting it in the closet. And Florence! Heaven forbid there should be anyone like Florence anywhere. Always teasing Molly maliciously, dreaming up new and more humiliating punishments. Like the one last week when Molly had to kneel on a freshly chopped piece of wood during the entire supper in front of all the womenfolk eating in the kitchen, splinters in her knees, and then being sent to bed hungry. Luckily Mr. Hunter and all the menfolk always ate in the dining room and so didn't see that humiliating punishment.

Florence always took delight in making a fool of Molly in

front of everyone, in sending her to bed without supper, not letting her do her homework. Probably she hoped that Molly would fail in school—probably she herself never had good grades in her days and resented Molly for that. She didn't know why Florence made life so hard for her.

What really puzzled Molly was the high esteem the villagers had for the Hunters; there seemed to be a myth surrounding that family. Of course, nobody knew of the cruelty that went on inside the house once the doors were closed. Nobody would believe her if she talked, and she would only get punished for 'lying.' She couldn't even write her mother about it because mother couldn't take her back until she finished school so she could start working for money. But thank God she didn't have to stay here forever; she just had to make the best of the situation.

Molly entered the house and sniffed. Something was cooking. In the hall in front of the kitchen there was a huge wood stove which was used only to make preserves of vegetables, fruits, or meat after a butchering. But this was not the season. The big, heavy iron kettle was on the stove and something was boiling away madly. No meals were ever cooked on this stove; it was too big.

"What's cooking on this stove?" Molly asked as she entered the kitchen. "It's not preserve time, is it?"

Mother Hunter shot a meaningful glance at Florence who was sitting at the table peeling potatoes. Florence just laughed her grating laugh and said nothing.

"What? What's the big secret?" When still nobody answered, Molly walked out to the stove and lifted the heavy iron lid. She couldn't see much for all the steam, but it looked like pieces of meat swimming around in greasy water. There was an unfamiliar smell.

"What is this? Is it supper? Why the big secret?"

"Well, since you must know," Florence finally answered, her horse face contorted in anticipation of some weird pleasure. "It's Stubby."

Molly stood frozen to the spot. Her eyes swam. 'No—oh no— it can't be true,' she thought, her mind going blank. Her knees were giving way from under her and she held on to the doorjamb. 'Nobody butchers their own pet,' she tried to rationalize, 'not even the Hunters.'

"You—you are joking, of course," Molly finally managed to say after scrutinizing the faces of the two women. Nothing seemed different. It had to be one of Florence's cruel jokes. It was just what a twisted mind like hers would dream up.

"You don't believe me? Why don't you go look for him? I tell you—it's Stubby, all right."

Panic took hold of Molly. She rushed out of the kitchen to look for Stubby. He was not in the house, not in the yard. She called all through the barn, looked behind the chicken coop and in the laundry shed. He was nowhere. None of the farmhands had seen him.

"I heard they were going to put him down today," one of them said without looking at Molly.

Then it was true. God Almighty! Molly's stomach heaved. She ran back to the house and lifted the lid off the kettle again. Just pieces of meat and bones and lot of grease. She was trying to fight that sick feeling in her stomach. She turned to Florence.

"You—you cut him up?" Her voice was barely audible. Who on earth would cut up a dog and boil him? And what for?

"Don't be so sentimental," Florence said coldly. "Don't you know that dog grease is an effective remedy for ear aches?"

Molly had collapsed against the wall. Surely she would vomit any second.

"Stubby was so fat—we'll get at least two or three jars of grease out of him. It's just a matter of boiling it out," Florence continued in a normal, matter-of-fact voice.

"There isn't much dog grease on the market anymore—people just don't bother any more. So we'll be able to sell it for a good price," added rich Mother Hunter with a self-satisfied smile. She was a businesswoman through and through.

'I'll have nothing to worry about as long as my mother keeps on paying for me,' Molly thought in a sudden flash of rationale. Then her stomach finally revolted.

"You're a stupid girl, Mollina Tarin! Clean up that mess! Can't you see we're trying to get supper ready?" Mother Hunter thundered with a grim look. You could almost see the ice in her veins.

Molly had vomited. She was crouching on the floor, sobbing and retching. She couldn't seem to stop. If only she would wake up... It was just too awful. She wanted to die. Florence got up and grabbed Molly by the arms and dragged her up the stairs into Molly's room.

"No! Please don't do it! Please!" Molly cried. She had some horrible visions of Florence swinging a hatchet. But the spinster just flung her into a corner.

"There'll be no supper for you tonight! We've had enough of your childish and insolent behavior. To make such a fuss over a dead dog!" With that, Florence slammed the door shut and turned the key.

Molly just sat on the floor in the corner where she had been flung, staring. Everything about her was numb. Her body, her mind, her soul. Darkness fell and the eerie shadows of the moon started creeping up and down the walls.

Through a thick fog she heard loud voices downstairs. A man's voice. "Stubby—killing him—not your decision—WHY THIS…" It occurred to Molly that this was the first time she heard Mr. Hunter argue with Mrs. Hunter. Probably he hadn't known about it. "Horrible for the child—want nothing to do with this…" The front door slammed.

Molly pictured Mr. Hunter washing his hands in the traditional bowl of water, except that in the traditional story it had to do with a crucifixion. Probably he would go play cards with his friends down at the pub. They'd wonder why he was so angry, but they would never find out. Mr. Hunter wasn't one to talk much.

As for her, she would have to present a normal face to the world as usual again tomorrow, as if nothing had happened…

*   *   *

Reality Check

We spent New Year's Eve dining in a rustic Swiss restaurant just outside of town with some old friends.

The special festive menu was excellent, and a bottle of good wine increased everyone's level of happiness and conviviality. Thanks to modern technology, the lone keyboardist by a small dance floor sounded like an orchestra, and we danced our favorite cha-chas and jives and whatever other requests we came up with.

Upon finishing our fabulous dessert—a homemade crepe filled with homemade ice cream and surrounded by a hot fruit sauce and whipped cream—the 'band' played another inviting jive.

"Let's dance," I suggested. "He doesn't play that many jives."

"I prefer to sit this one out," my husband replied. "I need a little rest."

He had barely settled into resting when a lady approached our table. "May I be so bold and ask you to dance with me?" she asked my husband, quickly turning to me, adding, "If you don't mind, that is… If you mind, I understand, and I will not insist."

"No—I don't mind," I assured her. "But it's really up to him. If he wants to, go ahead!"

My husband got up and the two disappeared onto the dance floor.

"Now, isn't that interesting!" I said to my girlfriend Hilda sitting next to me. "Here he was too tired to dance with me, but lively enough to dance with a stranger! I guess that's husbands for you!"

Hilda laughed. "Have you never heard the story about the rooster and the hen?"

"No—please tell me!"

She leaned forward and, with a little twinkle in her eye, told me the story.

A youngish couple from the city visited a farm to buy some fresh eggs. The woman seemed fascinated by the rooster who sat busily on top of a hen.

"How often does the rooster do that?" she asked the farmer.

"Oh, several times a day," he answered, and continued counting the eggs.

"You hear that?" the woman challenged her husband. "Hear that?"

The husband pondered the point for a short while, then he asked the farmer, "Does he always do it with the same hen?"

"Oh, no," replied the farmer. "Always with a different hen."

The husband turned triumphantly to his wife. "You hear that?" he finally said. "Hear that?"

Hmmmm…

*   *   *

That's Greek To Me!

When young Alan had to struggle through Greek and Latin studies as part of a liberal High School education back in his native Hungary, he sometimes wondered just how useful all this was. Little did he anticipate that, very soon, it would reward him with life-preserving warmth and a hot meal.

Toward the end of World War One, young Alan was taken prisoner by the Rumanians and forced into hard labor, working on a new airport landing strip. Food was scarce, and the starving workers could hardly withstand the cruel winter. Their thin, tattered clothing was no protection against the howling winds and the sometimes raging snowstorms.

One day, the commander showed up and spoke briefly with the sergeant in charge, motioning to the prisoners. They both approached the pathetic, shivering group and the sergeant barked, "Any of you speak Greek? There's a hot meal in it for you!"

Alan remembered the many hours he recited Greek poems in school. Obviously, nobody in the staff quarters knew any Greek, or they would not resort to recruiting a prisoner for whatever task was necessary. Therefore, nobody would be able to test his knowledge.

"I speak Greek," Alan volunteered.

He was driven to staff quarters and led into a warm room. "I'm cold and hungry," Alan was brave enough to say. They covered his shoulders with a blanket, then shoved hot soup and a hunk of bread in front of him.

"Eat! Then we need you to question a Greek officer we captured. Can you do that, kid?"

"Yes, of course," Alan assured them between slurps and bites.

In the meantime, his mind was working feverishly. How much Greek would he remember? Would the Greek officer co-operate? If not, what would happen to him, Alan? In any case, nothing could be much worse than starving and freezing out in that field.

"Come on—we haven't got all day!" Alan was being yanked off his bench and pulled into a small interrogation room. The Greek officer sat proud and erect, with a defiant look on his face. A gentleman! Alan's heart sank. He could not imagine such an important person to co-operate with him, play along with him. All was lost before it even started.

"Ask him how many troops there are, and how far away they are," the commander ordered. Alan concentrated as hard as he could, but all he remembered was part of a poem he had learned. He assumed a hostile look and said in a stern manner, in the best Greek he could muster:

"I come to pluck your berries harsh and crude,

And with forced fingers rude,

Shatter your leaves before the mellowing year."

The Greek officer stared at him in disbelief. Then, with a slightly hesitant voice, he quoted the next lines in Greek:

"Bitter constraint, and sad occasion dear,

Compels me to disturb your season due…"

"What did he say?" the commander wanted to know, impatiently.

"He said there are less than 200 troops, about ten kilometers south-west," Alan answered.

"Ask him what kind of artillery they have, and if it's all functioning," the commander instructed. Alan continued in his most authoritative voice:

"He must not float upon his watery bier

Unwept, and welter to the parching wind,

Without the meed of some melodious tear."

The Greek officer thought for a while, perhaps thrown off track by the missing part of the poem. Then, with seeming reluctance, he answered:

"Begin then, sisters of the sacred well

That from beneath the seat of Jove doth spring,

Begin, and somewhat loudly sweep the string.

Hence with denial vain, and coy excuse; …"

"What? What? How many?" the commander questioned.

"He said that they had three tanks, but two broke down," Alan invented. "There are four machine guns, and the rest just rifles. Not much ammunition left."

Suddenly there was gunfire outside. The commander rushed to the window, then turned around abruptly. "You two stay here—don't you move," he shouted and rushed outside.

They looked at each other silently, sizing each other up, Alan unshaven in tattered, shabby clothes with a blanket over his shoulders, the Greek officer very erect in a proud uniform. Two unequal men, somehow bound by Greek poetry. Finally the officer asked a question in Greek.

Alan shrugged his shoulders and shook his head; he didn't understand Greek. A slow, understanding smile spread across the officer's face, and for a flicker in eternity they were equal. Then the officer turned away.

The door opened. "Take the Greek back to the cell," the commander ordered his aide. "Then take the kid back to the field, as soon as the situation outside is under control. Oh—and give him more hot soup, if he wants more."

As Alan was hungrily slurping more hot soup, he wondered what would become of the Greek officer. What would they do to him once they found out that his information was 'false?' Or was it? Strangely enough, that brief moment of conspiracy in the interrogation room felt almost like bonding…

Just then, the commander stuck his head back in the door. Turning to Alan, he said, "You did well, kid," then rushed back out.

*   *   *

Many decades later, this brave and resourceful teenager became my father-in-law.

*   *   *

Danny Boy

It was a lively group of seniors, enjoying the merry boat ride on the tiny lake somewhere in the New York State hinterlands. Ranging in age from about 60 to 80, they had arrived from Canada by bus a couple of days earlier and had really brought a different dimension to this cozy, family-run resort.

Tonight was Talent Night, and several seniors had signed up to participate. Old Joe had brought along his harmonica, and Nellie with the pinkish hair was going to perform an old Vaudeville routine. Little Marvin with the peg leg was practicing a short comedy routine, while Bobby, a jolly Irish fellow, was going to sing. Ben and Gloria dusted off a hilarious 'bickering couple' sketch that they had performed a few times in retirement homes in Canada.

During supper in the dining room there was a happy and expectant atmosphere. Nellie created quite a stir when she entered, already dressed in an outlandish Vaudeville outfit, her pink curls piled coquettishly on top of her head. Diminutive Marvin, sitting at her table, kept pulling up his trouser leg to show off his peg leg that, it appeared, had seen better days.

Irish Bobby broke into song between the soup and the main course. "Hey, Bobby, wait 'til you're on stage!" boisterous Ben yelled across the room. "Don't spoil our dinner!"

"Oh, be quiet, you pre-historic expert in flatulence," his wife Gloria countered, starting the 'bickering couple' routine in earnest, much to the amusement of the other dining room guests.

After dinner, everyone assembled in the main lounge, scrambling to find seats with a good view of the stage. Old Joe was warming up his harmonica as quietly as he could, while Nellie the Coquette was practicing smiles into her hand mirror, hoping in vain to minimize her considerable wrinkles.

Finally, the lights dimmed slightly. "Ladies and Gentlemen and Others," the MC hollered to quiet down the crowd. "Tonight we have an excellent show for you! Our talented performers range in age from 11 to 78 years, and you'll love them all!

"How about we start with the youngest—Tracy—where are you? Come on up here, sweetie! Ladies and Gentlemen, here is 11-year-old Tracy who will dazzle us with her favorite Irish jig!"

A youngish woman coaxed a slender, self-conscious girl with long golden locks onto the stage. "Don't worry—you'll be great!" she whispered to her. The girl kept her eyes downcast, but the moment the music started, she straightened up, threw her head back, and started dancing magnificently. At the end, she shyly accepted the thundering applause and returned to her seat.

Old Joe was next. He spit into his hands and slicked back the few strands of yellowing hair he had left. Then he sat down on the stool on stage and, tapping his toe, launched into a sexy, rhythmic blues on his harmonica. The audience went wild.

Little Marvin limped onto the stage, rattling off a string of funny one-liners. Then he pretended to be attacked by an imaginary big bully who didn't like his jokes, and Marvin started shadowboxing with him, kicking him with his peg leg until the bully lay defeated on the floor.

Next, Nellie the Coquette sauntered on stage, swinging her hips and fluttering her false eyelashes. "Hey—Nellie! You forgot to iron your face!" shouted Ben, always eager to be noticed.

"Oh, shut up, Ben—it's not your turn to perform yet!" Nellie defended herself. Then the music started and Nellie did a lovely ballroom dance routine with an imaginary partner, surprisingly keeping her balance through it all. The audience was charmed.

Then Ben and Gloria kept everyone in stitches with their funny, incessant, and sometimes mean bickering, the kind that many people could identify with.

Irish Bobby came on stage last. He loosened his belt buckle a notch and wiggled his soft belly into a comfortable position. Then he took on a dramatic, almost operatic stance and sang "Oh Danny Boy" with typical Irish sentiment. When he came to the line, "If I am dead, as dead I well may be, Ye'll come and find the place where I am lying… " his voice wavered, and he quickly wiped a tear from his eyes. By the time he finished the last line, "And I shall sleep in peace until you come to me," there was hardly a dry eye in the house.

Next morning, another beautiful day was dawning. Despite

her relative success on stage, Nellie the Coquette had not slept well and was up early, looking quite a bit worse for wear, her pinkish hair tied carelessly back in a bun. Without make-up, her generous wrinkles were even more prominent, and the old tracksuit did not flatter her much.

On her way back from an early morning walk around the property, she decided to cross the lobby on the way to her room. Most people were still in their rooms, and the lobby was deserted. Then she saw Irish Bobby sitting in the rocking chair, dozing, one hand over his chest.

"Hey, Bobby—time to get ready for breakfast," she shouted cheerfully. Bobby didn't stir.

"Hey, Bobbie—wake up!" When he still didn't react, she went over to him and shook him by the shoulder. He slumped forward, and she had to catch him from falling off the chair. His body remained in a strange, bent-over position, as if frozen.

She started screaming. "Help! Somebody! HELP!" The young night clerk came running, buttoning his jacket. Together, they got the cold, stiffening body back into a sitting position. "He did have trouble with his heart," she muttered to herself. The desk clerk covered Bobby with a blanket and called the appropriate authorities, while Nellie tried hard not to give in to hysteria

By the time the local ambulance arrived, some of the other guests started coming down for breakfast, wondering what the large blanket on the rocking chair was hiding. Then they glanced curiously at Nellie who was rocking back and forth with a glazed look, softly singing,

"Oh Danny Boy... oh Danny Boy... If I am dead, as
dead I well may be... Ye'll come and find the place
where I am lying... ahhh... And I shall sleep in peace
until you come to me..."

*   *   *

Senior Moments

Janos had been looking forward to his annual trip to Poland for some time already. Not only was he immensely proud to be invited back every year to address the student body at a renowned university in Warsaw, but he also planned to attend some cultural functions while in his native land.

He pored over his lecture material, making sure to cover all relevant points without repeating exactly what he had discussed the year before, just in case some of the same people were attending again this year. He practiced different stances in front of the mirror, rehearsing certain gestures he felt were particularly effective. 'Not bad for a 73-year-old boy,' he thought as he arranged his still lush gray hair, pulling in his developing paunch to admire his tall, fairly imposing stature.

He studied his 'TO DO' list carefully: after all, he didn't want to goof again, as he had done a few times lately. 'Senior Moments' his wife loved to call them, and he hated that term. After all, he had a brilliant mind, and such incidents should be termed 'absent-minded' rather than 'senior moments.' Yes, he was a senior, but he was not old—not yet.

He cringed as he remembered the last piano recital he attended. He had bought an expensive ticket for the best seat in the house a few months earlier—just one ticket, because his wife was not interested in classical music. Then, a week before the event, he rushed out to buy a ticket because he didn't want to miss his favorite pianist, totally forgetting that he already had an excellent ticket. This time, however, only some cheap seats were still available.

At home, he realized that he now had two tickets for the same recital. He decided to keep the expensive ticket and phoned a friend who was willing to buy the cheaper ticket from him.

The night of the concert, Janos was led to a seat at the back of the top balcony, on the side. Hey—wait a minute! There must be a mistake! He checked his ticket: no, there was no mistake. He had given his friend the wrong ticket! So, while his friend had paid peanuts and enjoyed the best seat in the house, Janos sat cramped and miserable in his cheap seat way up in the peanut gallery—for which he had paid a small fortune. A painful 'senior moment' indeed!

His wife still teased him about that, especially since he lost money on that deal, and he had a reputation for being a tightwad. And whenever she wanted him to spend some money on her, she also loved to remind him of his various duplicate and triplicate sets of CDs—identical CDs because he kept forgetting that he already had them when he bought more. He invariably tried to sell them to his friends to get some of his money back, but that didn't always work. 'My senior moments are getting too expensive—I can't keep repeating them,' he said to himself.

However, there had been times when, sly fox that he was, he had managed to salvage some of his money. Once he had sold some expired tickets for a draw to an unsuspecting friend when the draw had taken place a week earlier and the tickets had not won. The friend had trusted him and had not checked the draw date until a few days later, but then was too diplomatic to say anything.

The lecture at the university in Warsaw had gone well. Although all students were Polish, Janos spoke in his heavily accented English simply because he was not familiar with all those technical expressions in Polish, having left his homeland as a young man. He packed up his notes and headed back to his modest hotel. He was looking forward to seeing the much talked-about play, The Moon Also Rises, which apparently was a must-see.

Although tickets had been sold out months ago, he had bribed some hotel clerk to find him a ticket, by hook or by crook, and it cost him a small fortune. But he had his ticket! He didn't know what the story by this famous playwright was all about, but it had been playing for two years now to rave reviews.

At the theater, his seat was one of those emergency fold-down contraptions in the aisle—terribly uncomfortable, especially for a man his size, but he was willing to suffer for the sake of culture. The play began.

After just a few minutes, a strange, uneasy feeling swept over Janos. He tried to remember... Yes! It was the same play for which he had managed to get an expensive ticket during his visit last year, and he had hated it! In fact, he had hated it so much that he had walked out after only 15 minutes. And here he was again!

He looked at his watch: it was only seven minutes into the play. Should he walk out now? Or should he wait another eight minutes to leave at the same time as last year? For all that money?

Squeezing himself out of his cramped seat Janos got up, and his seat folded shut as he walked out. Well, there was another expensive senior moment, but this time he would not tell his wife.

*　　*　　*

The Perfect Solution

"Come on over—I just made the most wonderful cheesecake," my friend Paula enthused over the phone. "My husband says it's my best one yet!"

So, later that day, I dropped in for a visit. Paula was known for her interesting cooking and delicious baking, so I was looking forward to that "best yet" cheesecake, even though my waistline didn't really need it.

Her large dog, Spotty, a beautiful Dalmatian, greeted me as enthusiastically as ever at the door, after his dutiful, ferocious, initial barking. "Let me make some tea, and then we can have a slice of this heavenly cake," Paula said. "And we can have some girl talk—Terry is not back yet from his dentist appointment."

While the tea was steeping in her lovely, hand-painted teapot, she showed me her new curtains that had just arrived for her newly renovated bedroom windows. "Don't you just love that color!" she gushed, and I cringed inwardly. They were a horrid taupe-purple, the same color as her husband's car that I had always detested. "How interesting," I managed to say with some faked enthusiasm, and I realized, once again, how very different we were in matters of taste.

Finally, we sat down to tea, and Paula served me a generous slice of that well-promoted cheesecake. I took a bite and nearly choked. It was salty and a bit rubbery, almost stringy—how could she! I tried to smile bravely, hoping that she might interpret my bulging eyes as appreciative, while trying to swallow that revolting piece of what passed for cheesecake. I gulped down my tea to get rid of that awful taste in my mouth. What was I going to do with the rest of that salty rubber on my plate? How could I not eat the rest without hurting her feelings?

"Well, Paula—you have really outdone yourself this time," I finally said, very sincerely.

"Isn't it incredible? Even the dog loves it!" Paula was beaming as she patted Spotty on the head. Well—didn't she know that Dalmatians will eat anything, that they are the garbage cans of the dog world?

But that gave me an idea. "Paula," I asked, "didn't you say you got another funny story on the Internet?"

"Oh, I'm glad you reminded me—let me go to the computer and print out a copy for you," she said. "You don't mind waiting?"

"No, go ahead," I encouraged her. "I'll finish my cake in the meantime."

As soon as Paula left the kitchen, I motioned Spotty over to my chair. He had been staring at the cake and at me all along. Now he saw his chance to get his share.

I put my plate on the floor in front of him, and he devoured the entire piece within seconds. Contentedly licking his chops, he went back to his corner and gave me a grateful look. I quickly put the plate back on the table and crumpled my napkin onto it.

As Paula returned to the kitchen with the printout, I gave a huge sigh of satisfaction, patting my tummy. "Boy—that was really filling," I said. "No more food for me today!"

"Well, I'm glad you liked it," Paula said benevolently. "Here's your funny story; I hope you enjoy it as much as the cake!"

On my way out, I patted Spotty on the head. Was it my imagination, or did he really give me a look of complicity? 'This could be the beginning of a beautiful friendship,' I thought, as I wiped a last telltale crumb off his nose.

Then I kissed Paula good-bye and headed for my car.

*   *   *

The Tactic

The two friends had been driving behind an older black van for a while now, wondering why it slowed down sporadically and wavered from side to side regularly.

"Another one of those bad drivers," Alyson remarked to her friend Betty in the driver's seat. "Makes you wonder how they ever get their license!"

They were approaching the electronic toll highway, hoping that they would finally be able to overtake that annoying van. As they got close to the access, they noticed the back doors of the van opening a crack.

"What on earth!" Betty muttered. "How did that door open? There was no bump in the road!"

Just then a tiny hand fell limp under the door frame, partly onto the license plate, and dangled there.

"My God—is there a child's body in that van?" Betty handed the cell phone to Alyson. "Maybe we should call the police!"

Just as Alyson was going to press 9-1-1, the tiny hand moved back into the van, and slowly the door closed again. The whole incident had taken place almost imperceptibly.

The two friends were stunned into silence for a while. "What was that all about?" Alyson asked. But since they couldn't make any sense of it, they soon forgot about it.

The following week, the two friends were having their usual salad and sandwich at their local luncheon counter. "Well—I'll be… look—read this!" said Betty, pointing to an item in the newspaper. "Do you remember that strange black van last week?"

According to the newspaper, an unmarked police car happened to drive behind an older black van as they were both entering the electronic toll highway. The door of the van opened a crack, a child's hand slid down over the license plate to cover it enough to obscure it from the electronic reader overhead, then moved back into the van, and the door closed.

The undercover policeman realized that the whole thing was just a tactic to avoid the license plate being recorded by the electronic reader, and therefore to avoid the toll charges. The police car overtook and stopped the van, and the driver was charged.

Upon questioning, it turned out that the driver had trained his little daughter, on his precisely-timed command, to open the van door very gently and almost imperceptibly, to cover the license plate as much as possible with her little hand, and then, again on his well-timed command, to withdraw her hand slowly and close the van door.

"What some people won't do to save a few dollars," said Alyson, shaking her head. "It seems hardly worth while, considering the consequences when you get caught."

"What bothers me much more," added Betty, "is what lasting effect this sort of criminal training will have on the little girl. Can you imagine her as a teenager?"

"More than a handful, I would say," concluded Alyson. Then they paid their bills and went back to work.

* * *

The Amazing Jack Crow

Jack was certainly a most unusual neighbor, with strange habits. Having no fixed address, he preferred to live out in the open and roam around in the nearby ravine, talking to trees and taking refuge in bushes. Although generally friendly, he hated dogs and was a bit shy around people.

Owen, one of our neighbors down the street, was probably Jack's closest friend. Whenever Owen wanted Jack's company, or introduce him to someone new, he would whistle the first bar of a certain tune, and Jack would suddenly, silently, appear out of nowhere, using his own stealth methods.

Jack would then dutifully bow to the newcomers and proceed to pick the lint out of any unsuspecting trouser cuffs. Then he and Owen would go sit on the front steps, or in the back yard by the pool, and tell each other tall stories, punctuated by Jack's occasional horrific screeching to underline some undoubtedly salient point.

We first met Jack on one of our after-dinner walks, in late summer. He and Owen were watching another neighbor digging up his yellow lawn patches to expose armies of well-fed grubs, and Jack decided to pitch in and get rid of all those squirming, fat grubs, displaying considerable gusto for the job.

As we were experiencing the same grub problem on our lawn—along with many other neighbors—I was seriously contemplating hiring Jack the following year, if necessary. We had just paid some serious money to a lawn specialist, and we speculated that Jack would be a lot cheaper and probably more effective, even though his work habits were not too predictable. He tended to come and go as he pleased.

But fate intervened, cruelly and unexpectedly.

In December, during one of his excursions into the ravine, Jack was viciously attacked and killed by a hawk. Owen, whose house backs onto the ravine, heard his terrified screams for help, but he was too late.

He brought Jack's twisted little body back up to the house, wiped off the blood, and lovingly brushed the feathers until they were, once again, black and shiny. Then the family gave Jack a solemn burial at the edge of their back yard, by the ravine.

The following Easter, Owen's family added another painted egg to their permanent Easter egg collection:

R. I. P. Jack Crow

May—December 1995.

Our unusual neighbor, Jack the crow, is no more.

*   *   *

Falstaff

John Wilson settled himself comfortably into his red plush seat, pulled the pleats in his dark trousers straight and loosened his belt by just a notch, making sure that no one had observed his last act of non-etiquette. Then he carefully smoothed his hand over his thinning hair, checking that his small bald spot was still meticulously covered.

It was another ten minutes till curtain time. In his row, most people had already taken their seats so he didn't have to get up again for latecomers. He looked around for any familiar faces; although it was Wednesday night, the theatre was filling fast. Over in one of the loges he saw Mr. and Mrs. Ryan; they smiled and waved. They would wonder why the seat next to him was empty, why Elena was not with him. John strongly disliked the idea of having paid such good money for an empty seat.

Elena might still come, he thought. She had promised to rush over if the PTA meeting was finished early enough. She might make it for the second act. Why couldn't she for once skip that meeting? He himself never went, of course. He was so busy with work; he often had to take papers home to finish a project. He certainly had no time to attend boring meetings where the various mothers complained about conditions or bragged about their children's performances. At first, Elena had nagged him about his duties as a father, but now she didn't bother any more and just went alone. Although sometimes it amused him to listen to the gossip Elena brought home, he never asked her what went on at those meetings. He felt that Peter's grades were Elena's business, and paying off the mortgage was his.

The musicians started tuning their instruments. John leafed through his program. Falstaff, by Giuseppe Verdi. He smiled. The name Giuseppe Verdi sounded so melodic, but translated into English it simply meant Joseph Green. John was not familiar with the opera Falstaff, so he read the outline of the plot. The cast sounded fantastic: baritone Louis Quilico as Sir John Falstaff; soprano Clarice Carson and contralto Maureen Forester, among the better-known ones. John was really looking forward to a great musical evening. Too bad Elena wasn't here, he thought, but then she was not as keen on serious music as he was.

A hush fell over the audience as the Maestro took up his position at the podium and led the symphony orchestra through the overture. Then the scene opened with the beer-bellied, ridiculous figure of Sir John Falstaff plotting to seduce a married lady by the name of Alice Ford.

John chuckled. He couldn't imagine Falstaff seducing anyone with his two-inch fringe of unruly red hair growing from ear to ear, framing a large pink pate, a pair of bushy eyebrows shooting up angrily towards his temples. Below his pear-shaped body, his legs looked like toothpicks all dressed up in boots. What woman in her right mind could possibly be attracted to such a comic shape of a man? And yet, Falstaff reminded John of somebody—somebody in his neighborhood who had the reputation of a Don Juan. For the moment he couldn't remember who, so he just pushed the thought out of his mind and concentrated on the action on stage.

John decided not to leave his seat during the first intermission so that Elena could find him more easily. He saw the Ryans leave the loge; probably they would expect him out in the lobby or at the bar, but he would wait for Elena and meet them during the second intermission. He was getting annoyed again. Why did Elena embarrass him so? She knew how he liked to keep up appearances. An empty seat beside him was definitely not good for appearances, especially when neighbors were watching. First Elena had promised to accompany him, but then insisted in the last minute that she had to attend this particular meeting because there had been a sudden drop in Peter's grades that needed discussing now. He hadn't noticed any change in Peter, but he had to admit to himself—and only to himself—that he really didn't spend enough time with his family to notice.

The lights dimmed and the seats were filling up again. Thank God he sat near the middle of the row or else he would have to straighten his trousers umpteen times. He checked his hair again; some people were so carelessly moving around in the row behind him. Boors! He made sure that the handkerchief in his breast pocket still showed exactly half an inch, the way he liked it.

The melodious music and the rambunctious Falstaff put John in a better mood again. That fellow was as utterly self-confident as he was ridiculous! The audience broke into laughter when, in the second act, Falstaff came prancing down the stairs in his most elegant and elaborate clothes, all puffs and frills and feathers, ready to conquer Mrs. Alice Ford.

There was that resemblance again... Was it the prancing? The flashy clothes? John was trying to concentrate on the opera, but Falstaff's resemblance to someone kept nibbling at his mind. The similarity was annoying; it kept distracting him. Was it those wild eyebrows? Suddenly John remembered. Romeo Lamoureux! The new French teacher at Peter's school. A bachelor with a reputation. Elena had told him about Romeo, and they had both laughed and wondered if he was a swinger in order to live up to his name. Romeo had bought one of those tiny old houses in lower Westmount by the railroad track and lived there all by himself.

John remembered that Elena used to tell him all sorts of gossip about this French teacher, how the female teachers seemed to have an eye on him and how some of them had made it to his house. Then, one day, John and Elena met him on the street. John was surprised to see a slightly pot-bellied, middle-aged, half bald, perfectly average looking but likeable individual with bushy eyebrows, like Falstaff, and an over-abundance of self-assurance, like Falstaff. John couldn't figure out why women should swarm around him like moths around a light, but Elena said that, apparently, he had great charm and knew how to make a woman feel like a woman. To John, this sounded like utter nonsense; he didn't even pretend to understand that. To him, a woman was a woman, just like a man was a man, and that was that. He was not a man to understand women; he was a businessman. He felt that his quite sizeable salary was appreciation enough for any woman. What more did women want?

Probably Falstaff had the same charm as Romeo Lamoureux, a charm that he could not see.

On stage, the vain Falstaff had strutted into Mrs. Alice Ford's home, declaring his love to Alice without wasting any time. He's not one for much preamble, John thought. But already the arrival of Mr. Ford was announced and Falstaff was squeezed behind a screen to hide him from the wrath of a jealous husband.

Mr. Ford and his companion dispersed around the house to seek out the hidden would-be lover. Mrs. Ford sat prettily at her dainty desk. When the men were out of the way, Falstaff was stuffed into a laundry basket that was considered a more effective hiding place. Everyone chuckled when Mrs. Ford's accomplice had to sit on the basket to keep the lid on because Falstaff threatened to spill over. The men rushed back into the room, looked behind the screen, moved the rocking chair out of the way, and checked every corner.

Although the search for Falstaff was humorous, something again bothered John. He couldn't quite put his finger on what it was. When, in the highlight of the farce, the men picked up the laundry basket and pitched the contents out the window and into the river, John didn't join the laughter. His uneasiness grew; something was nagging him again and he didn't know what it was. He felt it moving around in his gut and working itself back into his brain. He could no longer enjoy the wonderful music, no matter how hard he tried to concentrate. He fidgeted around in his seat and tried to dismiss this strange anxiety.

During the second intermission, John determinedly left his seat and mingled with the crowd in the lobby. He had given up hope of Elena joining him this late; in fact, he was now angry with her. By the bar he met Mr. and Mrs. Ryan. He hated to face them because his temper was growing worse and he felt ridiculous being at the opera alone.

"John!" Mr. Ryan exclaimed, slapping a large, friendly hand

on John's shoulder. "We were hoping to see you at the last intermission!"

"I was waiting for Elena," John grumbled after having nodded a hello to Mrs. Ryan.

"Was she not feeling well—or too busy to come?" Mrs. Ryan inquired, not without a trace of malice in her voice.

That nosy female, John thought; always a bit malicious because Elena was slimmer and prettier. He gulped down a whisky on the rocks and said, "She didn't want to miss the PTA meeting tonight. It seems there has been some change in Peter's grades and she wanted that straightened out first. She was hoping to join me for the second act, but I guess things dragged on."

"The PTA meeting?—- Well!" For some reason, a strange look and an even stranger smile appeared on Mrs. Ryan's face. "The PTA meeting was cancelled tonight—didn't you know?" she announced with a voice that sounded like a trumpet. Her smile now seemed charged with meaningful implications.

John stared at her. "You mean—there was no meeting tonight?" He hated to ask, but he couldn't help it. What an ass he was making of himself!

Mr. Ryan tried to smooth things out a little. "She probably forgot about it and went." He sounded embarrassed by his wife's bitchiness.

"But then she could still have made it for the second act," Mrs. Ryan pointed out with obvious satisfaction.

"For God's sake, Myrna, be quiet! Don't mind her, John. I'm sure Elena has a good reason for not coming tonight. Don't worry."

John was relieved when the lights began to dim just as Mrs. Ryan was opening her mouth again. He watched her reluctantly follow her husband back to their loge for the third and final act.

John stood there, dumbfounded. He just didn't understand. Elena could have taken a taxi and been here an hour ago. How could she—oh, my God—the rocking chair!

Suddenly the fog seemed to lift from his brain and he realized what had bothered him in the second act—it was the rocking chair on the stage.

Elena had once told him that Romeo Lamoureux had a rocking chair in the living room and she seemed to find that very funny. She thought rocking chairs were strictly for old people who had nothing else to do all day but rock and twiddle their thumbs. When he asked how she knew about the chair, she explained that one of the female teachers at the school had told her. John believed her; he had no reason not to, although Elena was an attractive woman and Lamoureux was supposed to have an eye for the ladies. As far as he knew, Elena had never been to the French teacher's house—but now, he wasn't so sure. In fact, he grew ever more suspicious and upset that Elena hadn't come to the theater and that Falstaff reminded him of Lamoureux.

How did Elena know about the rocking chair? Was it possible that she had been unfaithful to him these past few months? Could she really have betrayed him? He, John Wilson, the upright citizen, the ambitious and successful young executive, many a lesser man's envy—he, a cuckold? It seemed utterly inconceivable to him, but what else was he to think?

Perhaps Elena never did go to those PTA meetings. Perhaps she spent those evenings with her Romeo, both squeezed into that rocking chair, rocking and laughing their heads off—laughing at him, the unsuspecting husband who worked late in his study without ever asking any questions. What a fool he had been! What a bloody fool! But Elena's luck had turned tonight because the Ryans happened to be in the theater, Mrs. Ryan being only too anxious to blow the whistle on her. Served her right.

John felt the blood pounding against his temples. People were bumping into him on their way back to their seats; the music was already starting again. In a sudden decision he rushed down the stairs to the garage and got into his car. In his infuriated mind, he was writing his own script to end the evening.

John was speeding along de Maisonneuve West, getting all the green lights. Fate is really against Elena tonight, he thought. She and her Romeo will think they have another hour together. Ha! He would set them straight!

But why was Elena suddenly unfaithful to him? She got everything she ever wished for. He was a good provider and never hung out in bars, nor did he gamble. He never looked at other women—well, not often, anyway. His secretary was well past her prime. In all the twelve years of marriage, he had never once sidestepped. That's what hurt his ego the most. If there was any sidestepping to be done, he should be the one to do it, not his wife. Maybe Elena felt neglected. This was one aspect of women he had never understood, but he had never spent much time thinking about it, either. Strange that it took Falstaff—or Lamoureux?—to force him to think about it… He had to admit that his executive position didn't allow him much spare time. He was too high up in the company's hierarchy to work just 35 hours a week, and yet not high up enough to take off early sometimes. Perhaps it was a case of the suburbia syndrome right in the middle of the city.

When John got into Westmount, he stopped at a phone booth to check Lamoureux's address and then sped to the tiny side street and parked the car.

The quaint old house was the last one on the street, right beside the tracks. Very clever, John thought. The noise of passing trains could easily drown out any squeals of delight from lady visitors. Perhaps this Romeo planned his moves according to the train schedule, so that not even his one and only neighbor on the left could possibly hear anything.

There was a light downstairs, probably in the living room— the one with the rocking chair. There was another light upstairs. John stood in front of the house, undecided for a moment. He suddenly felt foolish. He faintly realized that in the past half hour he had driven his mind deeper and deeper into an irrational groove. He had lost his executive calm. Perhaps he should just go home, wait for Elena to get back and talk this matter out in an adult, rational way. By that time he might calm down and decide on a more mature course of action. After all, he didn't really want to punch Romeo Lamoureux in the nose—what if Lamoureux was the stronger one? And once the story got around to his circles it would just be too embarrassing.

Now there was a movement in the living room. Because the curtains were drawn, he could see only silhouettes. One was on the corpulent side, obviously the French teacher. The other one was slim with hair to the shoulders. Elena! John felt another surge of jealousy and rage aching in his gut.

He moved closer to the window, straining to see more. If only he could catch them in a compromising position! But the faint light and the folds in the curtains made it difficult for John to distinguish any details. The slim figure was now sitting on the sofa and the corpulent one was standing behind the sofa, bending down. The two heads seemed to melt into one. How dared this Frenchman kiss Elena!

John pounded on the locked front door and kept pounding until the light in the hall was turned on.

"Mon dieu—ouat iz se madder?" Romeo Lamoureux demanded in his heavy French accent as he opened the door. He stood there in a silken gold-and-red robe and matching slippers, his bushy eyebrows two angry question marks.

But John brushed him aside and ran into the living room. The rocking chair in the corner stood empty. On the sofa sat a slim young man with shoulder-length hair, looking very surprised at all the commotion. There was a pile of books in front of him on the coffee table. A sketch of some sort lay unfolded in his lap.

"Where's Elena?" John shouted, confused and angry.

"Ooo? Ooo iz Elenaa?" asked Lamoureux.

"Elena Wilson, my wife. Where is she?"

"Monsieur—pleeze! Ow should I know ouere iz your wife?"

John remembered the light on the second floor and raced up the stairs.

He followed the light to a large bedroom-study. Three of the walls were lined with books and records—classical music, John noticed. A beautiful antique desk graced one corner, and a simple bed stood against the fourth wall that displayed a few tasteful paintings. There was an open book and a half-full glass under the burning lamp on the night table. But no Elena.

"Monsieur Wilson, you leef now or shall I call se poliss?" asked Lamoureux who had caught up with John.

"No—please," said John with a fallen face and sunken shoulders. He didn't know what to say. He felt such a fool. This Lamoureux seemed to be a cultured gentleman. He didn't dare look at him, but walked slowly toward the stairs.

"Okee Monsieur Wilson—you leef and I shall forget sis visit. I ope you find your wife," the Frenchman said, almost with compassion.

John drove home automatically. Elena had to be there—where else? But why? He was immensely tired; he was not used to wasting his energy in such foolish, irrational ways. Acting like a jealous teenager! My God—what if this story ever got around!

He found his son Peter lying on his tummy in the living room in front of the television. That boy was watching too much TV; perhaps this was the reason behind Peter's slipping grades.

"Have you finished your homework? You're watching too much TV," John said.

The boy looked up surprised. "Since when do YOU notice anything around here?"

"How dare you!"

"Well—it's true," said the eleven-year-old with a half sorry, half defiant look. "By the way—Mrs. Bloom called several times in the past hour. She said it was urgent. She didn't want to tell me what it was, though."

"Where's your mother?"

"Gee—how come she's not with you? Gosh, she forgot that the PTA meeting was cancelled and walked over to the school. Then she came back here in a mad rush and ordered a taxi to meet you at the theater. What happened?"

But John was already calling Mrs. Bloom.

"Mr. Wilson, thank God you called! We didn't know how to reach you! I didn't want to tell the boy! Oh, my God!" Mrs. Bloom sobbed.

"What are you talking about?" John interrupted her. "Calm down, Mrs. Bloom. Where's Elena?" Why did women have to be so hysterical? Why couldn't they be calm and rational like men?

Mrs. Bloom loudly blew her nose and took a deep breath. "Elena called me from the hospital—yes! No—not badly hurt, just shook up. She mistakenly went to the PTA meeting and then took a taxi -- she -- oh, she was so worried that you would be mad at her! She -- she said she nagged the taxi driver to go faster, and they had an accident on the way. Oh, poor Elena!" She blew her nose again. "She said the police insisted on taking her to the hospital. What? Oh—the Reddy Memorial."

"Thanks! I'm on my way!"

Poor Elena, John thought as he was driving towards the hospital. Here I'm worried about appearances while she gets into an accident because she doesn't want to upset me, and then I go accusing her of infidelity! What a louse I am... I don't deserve such a good wife. I'm not just an ass, I'm also a louse... But why would she be afraid of me? Understand women! After twelve years of marriage and... Tomorrow I'll buy her a big bunch of roses and she'll never know why, but that's all right. And I want to spend more time with her at home and taking her out—because some day she just might be unfaithful to me, and it will be my fault. But what a dumb thing to forget about the meeting. That's women for you! Couldn't she check with a neighbor? But—she is only human, so I should forgive her, I guess...

And Peter—I'll have to spend more time with him, too. The lip he gave me tonight! He should have more respect... But he was right. I haven't been concerned with things at home for years, blaming everything on my big important job. So what—someday I'll have a heart attack and won't even have enjoyed my family. Maybe this weekend we'll go somewhere, the three of us. It might take me a while to earn Peter's confidence, but I have to work at it before he turns into an impossible teenager... But I really ought to give him a licking for tonight so he'll know who's the boss in this house...

"I'm John Wilson, and I'd like to see my wife, Elena Wilson, please," John told the attendant at the hospital in his regained executive voice. He stroked his hair mechanically.

"Of course, Sir. She's under sedation at the moment, but you may sit with her. This way, please."

(1978)

I Danced With A Clown Today

Funky Lily the Clown looked her ridiculous best, in her lime green socks and blouse, her baggy red high-water pants patterned with tiny musical instruments, wide red suspenders, and a long-haired, wild, purple wig.

Today was the third day of her annual five-day participation in the grandiose RBC Jubilee, North America's largest professionally produced seniors' entertainment showcase, which always drew thousands of seniors and their families from across the province to the city's most prestigious concert hall. She was part of the lobby entertainment in the morning to welcome the crowds and put them in a happy mood before the fantastic stage show inside the hall started at one o'clock.

In the lobby there were bands playing on two opposite stages and groups of dancers performing. Funky Lily, as the self-appointed dancing clown, always checked out the crowds around the dance floors by the stages to find singles who were waiting, usually in vain, for someone to dance with. Most of them, male or female, were delighted to dance with a clown, because many had not danced with anyone for a long time.

One frail, elderly gentleman was looking for her every year, waving frantically upon seeing her, giving her a thousand-watt smile, hoping to dance with her. And Funky Lily always made sure to reserve one or two dances for him, trying to follow his nervous little steps and unsteady movements while making small talk.

Later, Funky Lily approached a very old lady in a back row seat who was nodding along with the music. "Would you like to dance with me?" she asked. The old lady beamed and nodded excitedly.

"I don't think so," a harsh, hostile voice answered for the old lady. The clown looked at the tight-lipped younger woman in the next seat. "NO—I DON'T THINK SO!!!" the younger woman repeated emphatically.

Funky Lily focused on the old lady. "But—would you REALLY like to dance?" she asked again. The old lady looked at the clown with pleading eyes and barely whispered, "YES!"

The clown turned to the younger woman. "Don't worry—I'll take good care of her—I'm very gentle with older people!" And she helped the old lady out of her seat and guided her safely to the dance floor. She put her arm firmly around the frail body, and they moved slowly and carefully around the dance floor. Whenever the old lady became unsteady, Funky Lily supported her tightly.

"I'm 92, you know," the old lady said, smiling happily, "and I haven't danced in many, many years! And I never danced with a clown before! Oh, this is WONDERFUL!"

When Funky Lily escorted her glowing partner back to her seat, she turned to the younger woman. "Thank you for allowing me to dance with your mother—it was such a pleasure for us both," she said to her. Then, reaching into one of her deep clown pockets, she added, "May I present you with this free CD of the band? It will be a nice souvenir of today."

How could the younger woman not smile, though reluctantly,

and accept the gift graciously, knowing full well that she had not given her permission earlier? Funky Lily squeezed the old lady's hand and left to dance with someone else.

About an hour later, someone tugged at her sleeve in the hallway. "Thank you again so much for dancing with me—I will NEVER forget it!" said the still beaming old lady as she and her daughter wended their way into the concert hall.

As they walked past, Funky Lily could hear the old lady repeat in a giggly sort of voice, "I danced with a clown today!"

*   *   *

REFLECTIONS

All that we are is the result of what we have thought.
The mind is everything. What we think, we become.
(Maharishi Mahesh Yogi)

Vacation Ponderings

No telephone, no bills, no cooking, no obligations; just relaxing, reading without interruptions, sorting out my thoughts, putting things in perspective, counting my blessings…

Contemplating my progress in some areas, my stagnancy in others; discovering new aspects of things important; discovering the new unimportance of previously important things; suddenly seeing the interconnectedness of previously unconnected things; realizing and regretting the enormity of injustices innocently committed…

Pondering the meaning of wise words on a page and mentally discussing them with a phantom spiritual friend; searching my soul for hidden, as yet undiscovered treasures to be mined and refined…

Reflecting on various loves in my life, both past and current, never to be forgotten; appreciating the wonderful men I have loved and still love, and being grateful that most of them have loved me back, pondering the lessons behind the heartbreak caused by some who didn't...

Observing the effortless coasting of graceful birds high above in the sky, simply allowing themselves to be carried by the flow of wind patterns, with only the occasional wing adjustment, seemingly or deceptively carefree—a true study in the economy of movement; but still needing to swoop down once in a while to dive for fish, or to find scraps of food, noisily fighting over a discarded delicacy with other birds—a sudden and total transformation from floating serenity to aggressive physicality. So very like humans, switching from calm contentment to sudden and sometimes violent aggression at the push of the appropriate button—bundles of contradictions...

From a window high above the water, observing a swimmer seemingly going through all the right motions but getting nowhere—oh, so like much of humanity, making the right moves to the best of their knowledge and ability, yet never getting anywhere, perhaps moving forward almost imperceptibly before being tossed back a distance by the inevitable wave of life...

Flirting innocently with a frail, 84-year-old gentleman, providing him with some now rare pleasure judging by the appreciative twinkle in his tired, old eyes, allowing him to reminisce about his younger and more handsome years, something to remember this—perhaps his last—vacation by...

And last but not least: trusting that the apparent raisins in that delicious rice pudding are not simply caramelized flies...

*   *   *

The End Of A Dynasty

During a recent visit into her past to spend some time with her old school friend Tyra in the hinterlands, Mollina Tarin happened to witness the end of the wealthy Hunter Dynasty. For over 130 years, the Hunter family had ruled not only the house, the only bakery and the only salt concession at a time when salt was sold loose by the pound, but also a large farm with much property, 26 cows, three horses, several pigs, and a sizeable chicken coop. In addition, for some years they also ruled the entire village when Father Hunter, the second generation in charge, was the mayor of that village of barely 2,000 souls.

Decades ago when Mollina was in their foster care, the old patriarch was the most influential man in the community, and her grim foster mother, Mrs. Hunter, was possibly the most self-important woman, ruling the female part of the household with an iron grip. Despite their wealth and standing, they greedily accepted Mollina's widowed mother's hard-earned cash for her room and board every month for years, although Mollina had to work hard both in the house and on the farm whenever she was not in school. Those facts, however, remained a well-kept secret for years.

During her four-year stay with the family, Mollina—or Molly, as everyone called her—was also exposed to the third generation of Hunters, sons and daughters ranging in age from about 16 to 28. The oldest son, Joe, was slated to take over the bakery and the farm, as the younger son was more academically inclined and left the family for further schooling as soon as he could. The three daughters would undoubtedly be married off. So, Joe was really the king of the roost and could do no wrong. As a young, naïve, developing teenager, Molly was fair game for him anytime and anywhere, as were other young girls who occasionally worked there or were foreign charity cases for a few weeks.

Later, after Molly's departure, Joe finally married and produced some children. Together with his wife and some employees, he continued the bakery, which he then passed on to his son Previn, the fourth generation Hunter and their only offspring interested in the business, who renamed the bakery "500 Degrees Fahrenheit." However, Previn was forced to give up the business for personal reasons and decided to lease the store and the bakery to an outsider.

So, after 130 years and four generations, this was the end of the Hunter Dynasty.

The transition from the Hunter Bakery "500 Degrees Fahrenheit" to the new, young "Manna from Heaven" owners took place while Molly was there on vacation, with the grand opening scheduled for June 4.

The day before the opening, Molly strolled through the cemetery to look up some familiar graves and came across the Hunter family plot. Four of them were underground so far: the one son she had never known; the second daughter who had died from breast cancer as a young mother; and her foster parents who had passed away ten years apart. Then she entered the handsome church where she contemplated the thousands of hours she had been forced to spend over the years. Afterwards she took a leisurely walk up and down the main street of the village and was amazed at the cleanliness of everything: the streets and sidewalks looked as if they had been freshly vacuumed and scrubbed. She had forgotten how devotedly people swept their stretch of street, the way she used to have to do it every Saturday. Then she stopped in front of her former foster home where the new employees were busy stocking the bakery on the ground floor and making last-minute preparations.

A large tent was set up next to the house with tables and benches, getting ready to serve special welcome drinks and goodies to sell at the opening next day. The house itself had undergone renovations over the years, with glass balconies now adorning the second and third floors.

Leaning over one balcony was an older man with grey hair and glasses, with his face turned away from Molly to watch the goings-on below. Could that be Joe? If it was, would she still recognize him after so many decades? She stood still, waiting for him to turn his face toward the street.

Suddenly he turned his head, and for the briefest moment their eyes met. Yes, it was Joe! She quickly turned away and walked on before he could recognize her, although he had no idea that she was visiting.

Molly had never wanted to meet him again, not knowing how she would react. And now so many painful memories came flooding back! She realized with a shock that these memories still held her captive, although she rarely ever thought of that part of her past any more. She was also shocked to realize that she had never forgiven Joe for the unspeakable things he had done to her so many years ago, when he was a horny young man with few if any outlets for the sexual urges of a normal young man, and she was a budding, developing teenager without any power, any rights, or any means of defence as a foster child.

'Get a grip,' Molly told herself. 'All these things happened not only in the last century but in the last millennium!' She had fairly successfully managed to suppress all that pain and shame, and rarely ever thought of it anymore. Now she was forced to realize that, for her own peace of mind, she had to learn to forgive him, as well as his mean and punishing mother—her dead foster mother—and his unbelievably cruel and sadistic older sister who had never missed an opportunity to make her life a living hell during her years there. She realized that, in order to cope and lead a normal life, she had simply swept everything under that comfortable old carpet and mostly forgotten about it.

Perhaps, now, the time had come to deal with all that ancient garbage under the carpet. Was that the hidden purpose behind her fairly sudden, almost impulsive trip into the past? Was it the necessary trigger forcing her to confront and finally come to terms with that most painful part of her life? And was it coincidence that it all happened at the precise time to witness the end of that dynasty?

Except that she didn't believe in coincidence...

What an auspicious opportunity then, Molly thought, to recognize and act upon the end of the Hunter dynasty as the end of its domination over her childhood memories, no matter how difficult this might be.

*   *   *

The Good Old Days

Whenever I hear older people talk about "the good old days," or complain that "things aren't what they used to be," I think: thank God they aren't! After all, what was so good about the old days, anyway?

Don't they remember the lack of comfort? The absence of hygiene? The ignorance regarding health issues, resulting in premature deaths? Kitchens devoid of any appliances? Washtubs and washboards instead of washing machines? The lack of private bath facilities?

Even coming from a civilized European country such as

Switzerland, I remember such 'good old days' very vividly, even if it wasn't all that long ago. OK—OK, yes, it was last century when I grew up there, but I don't know whether the conditions were much different in rural areas or small towns in North America, or still are in many parts of the world.

In my later teens I was living in Zürich, Switzerland's largest city and financial capital, in a typical old three-story house that had just one tiny toilet in the hall on the second floor that all occupants of the house had to use, day or night. You could have a cat wash in your kitchen sink, but if you wanted a bath, you had to go to a public bath facility where you were allotted a half hour to get clean, and then it was the next person's turn. Saturdays were the busiest days, of course, because people didn't have time during the week.

Although many old houses still have just one toilet on the middle floor, many individual parties have since added bathing facilities on their own floor. Newer buildings, however, have all the modern conveniences, of course.

So I wonder: Will my old boarding school, where I spent my first five years of schooling, have totally remodeled to accommodate modern demands?

I remember our dormitory for a maximum of 28 young girls that was at one end of two long corridors, and the toilets that were at the other end. This presented a real problem for girls who needed to get up during the night. The corridors were dark, without lighting, with closets all along one side of the walls. On top of the closets were small windows, and on moonlit nights we could see frightful shadows dancing on the opposite wall where the nuns had their bedrooms.

We were too scared to venture down those corridors, especially as we were not allowed to run past the nuns' quarters. We would sit up in bed and wait for another girl to wake up, so we could go in pairs or groups, bravely marching down the hall, hand in squeezed hand. But if no other girls woke up, we would fall asleep again, ending up in a wet bed the following morning. This would inevitably lead to gentle spanking, which of course was no cure for bedwetting. Lights in the hallways would have been more effective.

As far as baths were concerned, a monthly gentle scrubbing by the nuns was deemed sufficient. The 'bath room' had a large tub in it, and we were placed into the tub in twos, wearing hospital gowns that opened in the back. There the two of us sat, facing each other, while a nun reached under the gowns from the opening in the back, making sure that no flesh was exposed at any time, and soaping us down, then rinsing us down, all under cover. Then some towel gymnastics under cover got us dry.

The same kind of gymnastics had to be applied when undressing and dressing in the dormitory. We had to slip the nightgown over our underwear, keeping the arms inside, then undress completely under the cover of the nightgown before we could insert our arms into the sleeves. No flesh was ever allowed to be shown -- after all, this was a very Catholic boarding school, and they seemed to be training generations of female prudes. It would take decades to get rid of such prudish thinking and behavior, undoubtedly requiring a lot of patience and understanding on the part of future mates.

At least, each girl had her own sink. A double row of 14 sinks, back to back, divided the dormitory into two halves, and twice a day we would brush our teeth and do our cat washes in unison.

I still don't know how the nuns bathed, and some didn't seem to ever indulge. On young, very fat nun, Sister Maria Nunciata, fell into that category. We could always smell her approaching, her sour smell preceding her wherever she went. We speculated that she probably had difficulty reaching underneath her many fleshy folds, especially if she also had to wash with her hospital gown on…

When boarding school became too expensive for my widowed working mother, I was placed in a foster home in another part of Switzerland, in a village of about 2,000 people. Although this family was rich and influential, there was still no hygiene, nor any facilities that could have been considered modern for the times.

A wood stove was the only 'appliance' in the large, eat-in kitchen. Early every morning we had to start the fire to make the huge breakfast of hash browns and eggs and cook coffee for about a dozen people, including the farm workers. The womenfolk and children ate in the kitchen to remain close to the work to be done, and all the menfolk were served in the dining room. And so it went, year-in and year-out.

There was no toilet in the house. There was an out-house type installation in an adjoining shed, accessible from a connection on the second floor, and that pipe drained directly from the second floor into a dung water pit far below. In that same shed there was also a washtub where the dirty clothes were soaked one day and washed on a washboard and rinsed the next day, all by hand.

In the village there were no bathing facilities, neither private, nor public. At the back of the farm, just past the barn, there was a small slaughterhouse that was used maybe twice a year, and it contained a large tub that could double as a bathtub when it was not used for animals. But as it was awkward to get hot water to the tub, it was rarely in use. Besides, it wasn't safe for females of any age to take a bath there, with lonely farm hands and unmarried grown sons never far away. So, cat washes in the kitchen sink when nobody was around were the only way to cleanliness.

Ah, yes -- the good old days! It was quite an education to be thrown from excessive protection and extreme prudishness at a Catholic convent, to having to hide and run away from women-starved men in the primitive, male-chauvinistic countryside, all in the very impressionable pre-teen and mid-teen, powerless years.

About the only common thread between those two extremes was: YES, the lack of comfort, the absence of hygiene, kitchens devoid of any appliances, the lack of private bathing facilities, the ignorance regarding health issues, and so on…

Thank God that things aren't the way they used to be! And the good old days? Well, as far as I'm concerned, they've been an interesting learning experience, but now I'm much better off without them.

Good riddance!

*   *   *

One Light In The Dark

Ronnie seemed particularly shy and insecure for his age. He looked about 28 years old, with a blonde Afro hairdo, slight build and a charming smile.

Having joined a Square Dance Club for the winter, he was partnered with Molly, a more experienced dancer some years older. Although he was new to it all, he was light-footed and learned fast, and the age difference between them didn't matter at all. He began very quickly to trust Molly, although he remained too shy to speak to any of the others in the group.

At the end of each session Molly would ask him, "See you next week?" to which he would invariably reply, "I don't know—I'm not sure yet—I may have to work…" and she would promise to call him a couple of days before.

Ronnie was a former schoolteacher who had found it hard to cope with students and teaching, and so he had switched over to training to become a psychiatric nurse. Molly didn't think that this was a healthy choice for him, but then she remembered that the few psychiatrists she happened to know seemed to have chosen their profession to sort out their own personal problems. So she said nothing.

Molly made a habit of calling him every Monday to encourage him to come to class Wednesday, and every time he would hedge and produce some flimsy excuses not to come—excuses meant to be overcome easily. Slowly he would open up to her on the phone, and after about an hour of pouring his heart out he eagerly promised to show up in class. All he really needed was someone to talk to. Living alone in the big city with hardly any friends, with his family far away in another province, he found it extremely difficult to cope with life, he told her. He seemed to have built up a dam of frustration and hopelessness, getting caught ever deeper in his dysfunctional view of life, and with her background in social work, Molly was afraid that, without help and support, that dam might crack and break.

After a couple of months, Ronnie didn't need to be called any more. He came to class without having to be prodded, and he began opening up to others also. Everybody liked him, and the group became his family.

One day he mentioned that he found working as a psychiatric nurse in one of the major hospitals so stressful that he was thinking of going back to teaching. Molly was shocked and concerned.

"Ronnie, before you commit yourself to teaching again, just try to remember what caused you to leave in the first place," she reminded him. "You quit that profession for a good reason, and it may not work out better this time around. You may not want to go through that experience again. Please—don't sabotage yourself."

His unhappiness and indecision took its toll and he began losing weight. He confessed that, as a bachelor, he rarely bothered to cook himself a meal. So Molly bought him a large bottle of multiple vitamins with minerals, and he promised to take them regularly to supplement his poor diet.

The months went by, and Ronnie now showed up for class early every Wednesday so that they could talk. He was still too shy to ever call Molly, although he clearly regarded her as his friend, if not his surrogate mother. Without being too heavy-handed about it, Molly tried to instill some practical life wisdom into his existence of quiet desperation, hoping it would not be too late to start building some soul stamina.

Then came the March school break. Ronnie was deeply disappointed that there would be no class that week, and he wondered what he would do that Wednesday night. Molly reminded him to call her whenever he wanted to talk, or that they could meet for coffee to bridge the March break. Otherwise, they would meet again in class the week after.

A few days before classes were to resume, Molly's phone rang.

"Hello, I'm Ronnie's mother," a lady identified herself. "I wish I could meet you in person, because Ronnie always talked about you, and he really enjoyed having you as a dance partner. But we live in Quebec…"

"Oh, he is a wonderful dance partner," Molly enthused. But suddenly she realized what the lady had said, and she felt a tightening in her chest. "Please tell me," she urged, "why are you talking about Ronnie in the past tense?"

After a heavy sigh and with a shaking voice, the lady finally brought herself to say, "Ronnie is dead... He—he just couldn't cope any more... that class was the only thing he looked forward to all week... it was his one light in the dark of his life... and March break..." She sobbed.

Molly was deeply shaken. She had tried so hard to help Ronnie, to be his friend, to be there for him without smothering him, but obviously it had not been enough.

"In the hospital he had access to drugs, and he knew how to use them..." The lady's voice trailed off.

Molly understood. "I am so sorry," she managed to say. "Everybody liked him, you know... we will all miss him... I will miss him so..."

The lady cried. "I'm just looking at that bottle of vitamins you bought him—that was such a caring thing to do... thank you for caring and for being his friend..." Her voice broke off again, and she was sobbing. "He was 35, you know, and he never could cope... oh, what did I do wrong?" Now sobbing uncontrollably, she suddenly hung up the phone.

Now, every year at March break, Molly is reminded of her gentle and fragile dance partner who left this world far too early, and of the importance of being all we can be to our friends who need us.

*   *   *

Millia Vara, Centenarian

With the passing of January 1, 2000, I officially became a member of a relatively exclusive club, the Three Centuries Club, having lived in three consecutive centuries. But, God, please—take me now! I've had enough of living.

Yet, my beginnings were so happy…

When a midwife first slapped me into life on June 9, 1898, my father threw a big party for all the members of our gypsy tribe. After all, I was his first daughter after three sons! There was much drinking and fiddling and dancing and merrymaking for three days—I guess that's why everyone remembered it.

While all my family had flashing dark eyes, I had my paternal grandmother's gray-blue eyes and fair hair, which contributed to the celebrations. So I was named Emiliana after her, and my middle name Liliana honored my mother. But everyone ended up calling me Millia. MILLIA VARA.

Ours was a close-knit tribe. We traveled in caravans through Eastern Europe, never settling anywhere for long. Education was almost non-existent, but my father, whom I adored, was a great storyteller, and he could read and write. I begged him until he taught me, and soon I knew his few books of folk tales and poetry by heart.

We survived by entertaining. We would set up our wagons on the outskirts of a village or small town, and people came flocking and gawking. My father, a tall, muscular man with a seductive smile and a permanent twinkle in his dark eyes, played the violin like a virtuoso, while my mother, a slender, beautiful woman with long, lush, wavy black hair, danced and told fortunes. From an early age on I danced with her, and the town folk were enchanted by 'that blonde gypsy angel girl.'

When I was about nine, I started reciting poetry while dancing, and I learned to choreograph my movements to fit the poetry. Once I began to develop my female forms, my dances became very sensual, and I was reciting my own erotic poetry. The money we collected now started increasing steadily.

One day, when my mother had gone to a farmer to buy some

food and my older brothers were busy helping the local metal smith, my father started undressing me. "I'm going to teach you how to please men—but don't tell your mother," he said. "We'll surprise her when you're ready." He was very gentle, and because I loved him so, it was unbelievably exciting. But I had a nagging feeling that it was wrong… However, I didn't tell anybody, and we continued our love lessons for a few years.

It was a wonderful time in my life. Although winters could be cruel and lean, from spring to fall I loved traveling the countryside, exploring barns and haystacks, watching animals mate and give birth, riding horses, learning to tell apart wheat and barley and rye, running through fields full of wild flowers and butterflies, writing poetry, dancing, hiding from young men when it suited me.

Then, suddenly, war broke out. I was only 16, but my world fell apart almost overnight. I was no longer 'that gypsy angel girl' but now we were all called 'goddam gypsies' and I was labeled 'that blue-eyed gypsy whore.' Where before we were tolerated and somehow appreciated for what we did, we were now suddenly outcasts, and the persecution began.

Our tribe scattered. We all had to try and blend in with 'normal' people. My brothers cut their hair short and found work in neighboring towns, but my beautiful father with his dark locks and flashing dark eyes could not blend in—he could only be a gypsy. Our income dried up; nobody wanted to be seen around any gypsies for fear of reprisals from locals.

We were now living in a shack, trying to make ends meet. My father was doing odd jobs for anyone willing to hire a gypsy. One night he came staggering home, all bloodied, some bones broken, his clothing torn. He could barely speak.

"Millia," he pleaded, "my sweet Millia—you must leave!

They're coming to get us all, they said. I don't want you hurt. You're too smart and too beautiful. Please—leave!" I had never seen my father cry before, and it broke my heart. Our persecutors had finally managed to break his spirit.

My mother, trying not to show her fear, helped me pack my two dresses and some bread into a bundle, and in the dark of night I left the only family I would ever have. I never saw them again. Only much later I learned that both my parents had been killed. I never heard anything from my handsome brothers; I could only hope for the best and fear the worst.

The rest of my life is not worth mentioning. I walked to the next town and got work in a household. Blonde and blue-eyed, nobody could spot me as a gypsy.

I worked my way across Europe, aimlessly, sometimes spending some 'recovery' time with a moneyed gentleman. I could not become attached very deeply to any person; I had lost all the people I loved, and I didn't want to go through that desperate feeling of abandonment again.

In England I married a kind, loving Harry Flaherty who sent me to school to learn proper English to translate my poetry. How he loved my poetry! Especially when I danced to it. We moved to Canada, but after a few years our childless marriage ended. I took back my maiden name, started teaching belly dancing, gave poetry readings, and published some of my own poetry.

Being fiercely independent had its price, of course. I had few marketable skills, and poetry did not pay for my living expenses. Although I managed to keep my trim figure, as you can see, I was getting too old to belly dance. I mean, people were snickering. 'Look at that old woman belly dancing,' they said. 'Doesn't she know when to quit?' But as long as I could still earn a few dollars with it, I didn't mind the snickering.

Now I've been retired for a while, of course, and I live in a tiny apartment in a Seniors Residence. I hate it. I hate concrete. I hate living alone, but I can't live with anybody, either. Although I've always enjoyed a rich interior landscape, I do need people to talk with, sometimes.

On special occasions, I still dance and read poetry, just for the seniors in the Residence, and they enjoy it. When you get old, you learn to appreciate the little things in life—you learn to give thanks for small mercies. Besides, I'm rather an oddity at the Residence because I have never really told my story to anyone. What is there to tell?

The sad thing is that I have never truly loved anyone since my father… I long for my childhood. I long for my family. I long to live in the country, but all I can do is come to this little park a few blocks away. I need a walker now, but I refuse to stay in that concrete building any more than I need to.

Here in the park I met a new friend, Georgia, and I have told her part of my story. She is much younger, only in her eighties, and I'm not sure she's really a friend. I suppose she needs me as much as I need her, so we keep meeting, even though we always end up arguing about something or other. But, oh, I need her!

Dear God, please take me home. Remember me, God? Millia Vara? MILLIA VARA! I will be 102 years old this June, and I've lived enough.

Please, GOD? -- DO YOU HEAR ME?

* * *

Millia Vara suffered a pelvis fracture a short time later and was confined to her bed in that hated concrete building. She fell into a deep depression and finally went 'home' before her 103rd birthday.

(2001)

A Test Of Faith

Some insightful person once said that, to some extent, we influence—and are influenced by—everybody we meet. So I feel ambiguous about having caused a devout Catholic to question her faith. Quite unwittingly, of course.

She was expensively elegant and strikingly beautiful, with shoulder-length, light brown, wavy hair, delicate features, with skin like alabaster, quite unlike other Portuguese people I had met.

"I have been away in New York for two weeks, and I can't wait to get back to Lisbon," she said to me with a deep sigh. "It may be silly, but I have been terribly homesick!" She turned away again to look at the pure white billows of clouds obscuring the Atlantic Ocean, some 39,000 feet below us.

I was on my way to Switzerland, planning to stay in Lisbon for a few days before continuing on to Geneva, and I was delighted to be seated next to a native of Lisbon who would be able to give me some valuable information on how to make the most of my very limited time.

Her husband was a doctor, she explained, and he didn't have time to go with her to New York to visit her ailing sister. "I don't like New York," she said apologetically, then added with a shy smile, "I feel that God is not there."

"Do you feel God in Lisbon?" I asked, curious. In my mind, God is either omnipresent, or He/She is not at all.

"Oh, yes—I always feel Him in Lisbon, very strongly," she replied earnestly, with a glow on her face. She reached into her very expensive handbag and fingered some rosary beads. "We are getting close to Lisbon. Less than one hour to go."

As we began to descend and the sprawling city of Lisbon came into view, she could not hide her excitement. "How beautiful this city is!" she exclaimed. "I don't like to leave Lisbon, but I love to see it from the air. Oh, how beautiful it is!"

I was leaning over to look at the various sights she was pointing out to me. "People always talk of the seven hills of Rome," she said. "But look how Lisbon spreads over the Serra de Sintra mountain range! Look at the Moorish citadel on that hill! Oh, look at the Tagus River! And over there, the Monastery! Oh! Oh!" In her excitement, the rich and elegant doctor's wife became a little girl again, almost bobbing in her seat.

Suddenly, the plane touched down, very gently. "Another safe landing, thank God," I remarked innocently.

She stared at me, horrified. The blood drained from her face, and I was afraid she was going to faint. "My goodness, are you not feeling well?" I asked, worriedly. "What's the matter?"

Her hands were shaking. She reached into her handbag again and showed me a lovely crucifix made of rosewood and ivory. "I forgot to clutch my crucifix," she whispered, totally shocked. "When I fly, I always clutch my crucifix during the landing to make sure we land safely… May God forgive me -- I forgot!"

"The main thing is, we landed safely anyway," I tried to assure her, feeling a bit guilty about having distracted her. But the incident seemed to have shaken her faith severely, and she could barely regain her composure as we left the plane and said good-bye.

To this day I wonder whether her faith had suffered permanent damage, having had to realize that most people rely rather on a competent captain and his crew, who are surely guided by the Almighty, to land their plane safely.

*   *   *

The Scavenger

Today, I saw her again: young, mid-twenties maybe; slender to the point of appearing frail; ash-blonde, shoulder-length hair; a common but pretty face. Although she tried to appear self-confident, her movements were those of a frightened but desperate doe ready to flee at a moment's warning.

I had seen her once before, in a luncheon cafeteria. She was reasonably well dressed then; she could have been any of the countless secretaries of that office building. So when she sat down at a table that had just been vacated and started eating the leftovers off the two plates, I was shocked. I remember staring at her, watching as she carefully picked both plates clean, rinsing the bits of food down with water left in the glasses.

I couldn't take my eyes off her. She avoided my rude stare—thank God, because I felt like a voyeur—and continued to behave very naturally. When there was not a crumb left on the table, she got up and scanned the room for other plates with leftovers, but either the tables had already been cleared, or the people were still sitting there. Resignedly, she left the cafeteria and walked up the street, presumably to the next eatery.

Finally I recovered from my shock. Indignation slowly turned to understanding and sadness; I was sorry that there had been nothing left on my plate that I could have offered her.

How hungry she must have been to swallow her pride and

expose her situation to the world! I wondered how long she had been hungry before deciding on her drastic but logical action. Obviously, she had enough pride and self-respect not to resort to other, more degrading solutions, such as selling her body on the street. I wondered where she slept and how she kept herself clean.

I realized that she would have to rely solely on cafeterias and make a fast move to tables not yet cleared; she would never be able to do that in a restaurant. As her clothes were clean and in good condition, she seemed to care about her appearance, and she had to have seen better days.

As I was eating a quick muffin in a mall food court today, I saw her again. She headed straight toward the garbage bins and retrieved some Styrofoam hamburger containers, but they were mostly empty. She carefully picked some leftover crumbs from one of the boxes, then looked around for other possibilities.

I watched other people stare at her in shock and disbelief, their stomachs full of hamburgers and French fries, and I saw myself the way I had reacted the first time. How difficult it seems to be for well-fed working people to feel some compassion! I walked over to the young scavenger.

"Can I help you with something?" I asked.

She looked bewildered. "No ------- I'm just hungry," she finally said, defensively.

"I mean—can I buy you something?" I insisted. "A sandwich, maybe?"

"Ohhh...." She muttered, surprised. "Maybe... a vanilla shake," she decided.

"Nothing more nourishing than that?" I asked.

"No, just a vanilla shake."

While we waited for the milk shake, I wondered about her

strange choice. I would have expected some giant sandwich, or something equally nutritious. But then I realized that most leftover food would be parts of sandwiches, and that she probably hadn't had a milk shake in a long time.

As I counted my change, I watched her take a long, satisfied sip. "Thanks," she whispered shyly, then slid away.

There, but for the grace of God…

*　　*　　*

Year-end Reflections

As 2006 draws to a close and I'm reflecting back on the year that was, I have decided that growing older is a gift. I am now allowing myself to be the person I was meant to be, enjoying who I have become.

No, not my body! Sometimes I'm surprised to see my expanding waist (my former constant 24 inches now but a distant memory), my rounding tummy, and my—oh, well… And sometimes I'm reluctant to acknowledge that stranger some years past her bloom that lives in my mirror, but I don't agonize over it. Never would I trade my great life with a long-standing compatible partner, my wonderful friends, or my interesting life experiences for less wrinkles or a slimmer waist.

As I'm aging, I'm becoming kinder to myself, more forgiving and less critical of myself. I've become my own best friend, and I cherish that friendship. I don't scold myself for eating that delicious chocolate, or for cutting my hair short just because I've had long hair all my life, or for getting emotional when my heart overflows with love and joy and affection.

I am entitled to occasionally overeat, to be eccentric, even to be silly. I take great joy in entertaining others as Funky Lily the Clown or as Funky Santa, especially those incredibly grateful seniors in nursing homes and hospitals who are so appreciative of a tender touch. I have seen wonderful people leave this world without realizing the unexpected freedom that aging can bring—like my mother-in-law whose passing over Christmas last year at almost 98 years of age really drove home that point.

So who can tell me now not to dance, or laugh, or play on the computer well into the night, keeping in touch with friends around the world by e-mail? I will continue to dance joyfully when the spirit moves me, and to keep on ballroom dancing as long as my body cooperates.

Sure, as part of the life process, how could my heart not have been broken a few times when losing a loved one, or seeing a child suffer, or when a favorite pet needs to be put down, or when a beloved friend calls it quits? But I refuse to become jaded over it. Broken hearts are what give us strength and compassion and test our resilience—what doesn't kill you, makes you stronger, right? A heart never broken can be sterile, and its owner can be cold and callous.

And my laugh wrinkles are precious to me: they are the results of many years of ready laughter. So many people have never laughed because they have never realized or appreciated the absurdities of life, or because they take themselves too seriously, afraid to look like fools, to lose their dignity. As someone said,

GROWING OLDER IS MANDATORY
GROWING UP IS OPTIONAL
LAUGHING AT YOURSELF IS THERAPEUTIC.

Getting older means that I care less about what other people think. I will continue to call a spade a spade and not a digging implement. I have earned the right to have a different opinion and to be proud of my thinking process.

So, in case you wonder—yes, I like growing older and wiser and more mature. I like who I am today, although I will always be a work in progress. As I am not going to live forever, I will not waste time crying over what might have been, or worrying about what might still be. I will no longer waste my time with people who, for reasons of their own, refuse to accept the person I have become.

Isn't it better to enjoy life with all its ups and downs and grow old gracefully while we still have the chance, than to die young? After all, life is a marathon, not a sprint.

*   *   *

Funky Lily the Clown continues to create fun and joy in people's lives

WINDJAMMER AHOY!

Lilian Marton at the 'big wheel' on the
windjammer POLYNESIA

Lilian and George Marton
are keeping fun and fitness
in their lives with dancing

Lilian Marton in a reflective mood
with her favorite White Tiger painting
by Robert R. Copple

ISBN 142510814-8

9 781425 108144